Flawed and Faithful

A Collection of 50 Biblical Figures Who Walked With God

This book belongs to:

Copyright © 2025 by Willem Janse van Rensburg
All rights reserved.

No portion of this book may be reproduced in any form without written permission from the publisher or author, except as permitted by copyright law.
This publication is designed to provide general information in regard to the subject matter covered. It is sold with the understanding that neither the author nor the publisher is engaged in rendering any professional services. While the publisher or author have used their best efforts in preparing this book, they make no representations or warranties with respect to the accuracy or completeness of the contents of this book and specifically disclaim any implied warranties of fitness for a particular purpose.

Scripture quotations are from the ESV® Bible (The Holy Bible, English Standard Version®), © 2001 by Crossway, a publishing ministry of Good News Publishers. Used by permission. All rights reserved. The ESV text may not be quoted in any publication made available to the public by a Creative Commons license. The ESV may not be translated in whole or in part into any other language.

The information provided aligns with traditional Biblical accounts.
For names that had multiple possible meanings, the most common interpretations are included.

Book Cover by Willem JvR
Illustrations by Willem JvR
First Edition 2025

ISBN: 978-1-998552-17-7

Preface

The Bible has many examples of human failure, people falling short of God's expectations. Great men and women declaring their love and obedience to God, only to find their faith failing when facing challenges and suffering. In awe of the magnificence of the events in the Bible, we forget these men and women were human too, born into failure, falling short, just as we do.

Because of our sin and our rebellious stubbornness, we continuously question God's Plan. Fortunately for us, it is a path that is not dependent on our willingness to participate or our ability to contribute. He uses us despite, and often because of, our shortcomings. Through mercy and grace, He made provision for our failures on the Cross at Golgotha.

I trust this book will remind you that, while imperfect, <u>you have value and purpose in God</u>.

While developing this writing, I limited quoted Scripture and instead include references to where these characters may be found in the Word. I hope this will serve as motivation for self-study, so you can get to know them better.

While I encourage you to study each figure the way you choose, also try to reflect on these:

- **Make it Personal:** For each person, consider how you identify with their circumstances and reflect on the reasons for this.
- **Facing Personal Struggles:** How do the challenges or moments of vulnerability experienced by each character mirror the personal obstacles you encounter in your own life?
- **Exploring Faith in Adversity:** In what ways does each character's response to hardship inspire you to deepen your trust in God during difficult times?
- **Transformation and Growth:** How might moments of strife encourage you to embrace change in your own spiritual life?
- **Living Out God's Love:** How does the character's relationship with God change after experiencing God's grace, justice, and mercy, and how does this affect relationships with others?

I pray you find encouragement and a renewed strength to endure until He calls us Home.

Psalm 103:14 (ESV) - 'For he knows our frame; he remembers that we are dust.'

Willem

Adam

Adam means "man" or "earth" or "red earth."

Adam was the first human created by God. He was given the privilege of direct fellowship with Him. Formed from the dust of the earth, he was placed in the Garden of Eden to care for it. God gave him dominion over all living creatures, meaning he had control over creation and the responsibility to look after all creation. Adam was also responsible for naming the animals.

Seeing that Adam was alone, God created Eve from his rib as his companion. Together, they were to multiply and fill the earth.

Sin entered the world when Adam disobeyed God by eating from the forbidden tree. As a result, he and Eve were expelled from Eden, and Adam had to work the ground to provide food. He became the father of Cain, Abel, and Seth, and through Seth, his lineage continued to Noah and beyond.

Adam lived 930 years before he died.

Adam disobeyed God's command by eating from the forbidden tree. Through this one act of disobedience, he broke God's trust and rejected God's authority. It led to a breakdown in Adam's relationship with God, and his separation from Him. Adam chose to disobey God, and this choice had lasting consequences for all humankind, as death entered the world through this sin.

God breathed life into Adam and gave him dominion over all of creation. This was God's first blessing of humankind. Even after his fall, God did not abandon Adam. He showed mercy, clothed Adam and Eve, and promised them redemption through one of Adam's descendants, our Redeemer, Jesus Christ.

Genesis 3:8 (ESV)
'And they heard the sound of the LORD God walking in the garden in the cool of the day, and the man and his wife hid themselves from the presence of the LORD God among the trees of the garden.'

Genesis 1:28 (ESV)
'And God blessed them. And God said to them, "Be fruitful and multiply and fill the earth and subdue it, and have dominion over the fish of the sea and over the birds of the heavens and over every living thing that moves on the earth." '

ADAM'S HISTORY IS RECORDED IN GENESIS 1 TO 5.

 Eve

Eve means "living one." In Biblical context, it means "mother of all living."

God created Eve as the first woman, forming her from Adam's rib to be his helper and companion. Together, in the Garden of Eden, they worked the land and cared for creation. God blessed them to multiply and fill the earth, giving them shared responsibility as stewards of all He had made.

Eve walked with God in perfect harmony, experiencing a world without sin. Unlike anyone born after her, she was formed directly by God's hand. She spoke with her Creator face to face and joined Adam in naming the animals of the new world.

Tempted by the serpent, Eve chose to disobey God's command about the forbidden tree. After eating the fruit herself, she offered it to Adam, who also ate. This single act of disobedience changed the perfect world they knew, as both Adam and Eve then faced the painful consequences of sin entering creation. Eve was the first to endure the pain of childbirth, she witnessed hatred between her children, and she carried the knowledge that her choice had brought death into the world, including the murder of her own son. Our relationship with God and creation was forever changed by the choices made by Adam and Eve.

Genesis 3:6 (ESV)
'So when the woman saw that the tree was good for food, and that it was a delight to the eyes, and that the tree was to be desired to make one wise, she took of its fruit and ate, and she also gave some to her husband who was with her, and he ate.'

Even in judgment, God showed Eve compassion. He clothed her and Adam with animal skins and continued to care for them despite their disobedience. Eve received the honor of becoming the mother of all humanity, and God gave her a profound promise that, though she lost Eden, through her family line would eventually come the Messiah, the One who would restore what was broken and fulfill God's plan of redemption for all of creation.

Genesis 3:15 (ESV)
'I will put enmity between you and the woman, and between your offspring and her offspring; he shall bruise your head, and you shall bruise his heel.'

EVE'S HISTORY IS RECORDED IN GENESIS 1 TO 5.

Enoch

Enoch means "dedicated," "trained" or "disciplined."

Enoch was the seventh generation from Adam in the line of Seth. He was the father of Methuselah, who became known as the longest-living person in the Bible. Enoch lived for 365 years, which was relatively brief compared to others of his time.

Scripture notes that Enoch walked with God. This points to a close, faithful relationship with the Creator, showing a life of deep devotion. Enoch did not experience death in the ordinary way. Scripture simply states that "he was not, for God took him," suggesting God took him directly to heaven without dying.

The New Testament also mentions Enoch as a prophet who foretold judgment on ungodly people. He is one of only two people in the Bible, the other being Elijah, who were taken to heaven without dying. Enoch shows us it's possible to live close to God even in corrupt times. His short but profound life proves that the quality of our relationship with God matters more than how long we live.

Enoch lived during an extremely wicked time that eventually led to the great flood. Despite this challenging environment, he remained faithful to God. Scripture records no specific sins or failings for Enoch. As a descendant of Adam, he would have inherited a sinful nature like all humans. He likely faced strong opposition for his faith, living in a godless society. His legacy emphasizes his unwavering commitment to walking with God despite the corrupt world around him.

Hebrews 11:5 (ESV)
'By faith Enoch was taken up so that he should not see death, and he was not found, because God had taken him. Now before he was taken he was commended as having pleased God.'

Enoch enjoyed a meaningful and lifelong relationship with God. God honored Enoch's faithfulness by taking him directly from earth to heaven without experiencing death. This extraordinary blessing showed God's favor and approval of his life. Enoch's unusual departure from earth foreshadowed the resurrection and ascension of Jesus Christ, and the transformation promised to all believers.

Genesis 5:24 (ESV)
'Enoch walked with God, and he was not, for God took him.'

ENOCH'S ACCOUNT IS RECORDED IN GENESIS 5:18-24.

Noah

Noah means "rest" or "comfort."

Noah lived during a time of great evil, yet he remained faithful to God. A descendant of Adam through Seth, he was the only righteous man in his generation.

God commanded Noah to build an ark, giving him detailed instructions on how to accomplish this. Though he lived in a land where it had never rained, Noah obeyed and spent years constructing the ark while warning others of the coming flood. For this, he was mocked and ridiculed.

After the flood, Noah became a farmer and planted a vineyard. God established a covenant with him, promising never again to destroy the earth by water. Through his sons Shem, Ham, and Japheth, Noah became the ancestor of all nations.

Noah lived 950 years.

Despite witnessing God's judgment on sin and avoiding the destruction of humankind by God's grace, Noah failed to remain watchful in his personal behavior after the flood. When the waters from the flood eventually receded, Noah became drunk and lay uncovered inside his tent. This act showed a lapse in his personal conduct and led to dire consequences for one of his sons. His failure came shortly after his greatest triumph, showing us the danger of becoming spiritually complacent. Scripture also does not show any record of repentance for this lapse in judgment.

Genesis 9:21 (ESV)
'He drank of the wine and became drunk and lay uncovered in his tent.'

After the waters receded, God established an unconditional covenant with Noah that extended to all living creatures. Symbolized by a rainbow, God promised never to destroy the earth with water again. Through this promise, Noah again found grace in God's eyes, leading to a lasting blessing for future generations, including this one.

Genesis 9:11 (ESV)
'I establish my covenant with you, that never again shall all flesh be cut off by the waters of the flood, and never again shall there be a flood to destroy the earth.'

NOAH'S HISTORY IS RECORDED IN GENESIS 5 TO 9.

Job

Job means "persecuted" or "hated."

Job was a wealthy man from the land of Uz who lived with integrity, feared God, and avoided evil. His prosperity included seven sons, three daughters, and vast herds of livestock, establishing him as a prominent figure in the region. Beyond his wealth, Job earned respect as a community leader who generously cared for the needy.

God permitted Satan to test Job's faithfulness by having his possessions destroyed, his children killed, and his body afflicted with painful sores. Despite these tragedies, Job maintained his faith, famously declaring, "The Lord gave, and the Lord has taken away; blessed be the name of the Lord."

Throughout his suffering, Job engaged his three friends and, later, Elihu, in profound discussions about justice, suffering, and God's role in human affairs. When God finally spoke to Job from a whirlwind, He did not directly answer Job's questions but revealed His supreme wisdom and power. Job's story concludes with his restored fortune exceeding his former wealth, the birth of ten more children, and his life extending another 140 years.

Job struggled to understand his apparent unfair treatment and suffering, at times believing his righteousness should have spared him such pain. Initially responding with remarkable faith, his conversations revealed increasing frustration as his ordeal continued. His laments signified the raw human response to profound loss. Job's desire for an audience with God to plead his case directly could be interpreted as presumptuous, and his desire for vindication occasionally overshadowed his trust in God's ultimate wisdom.

Job 3:3 (ESV)
'Let the day perish on which I was born, and the night that said, "A man is conceived." '

After Job acknowledged his own limitations and God's sovereignty, the Lord restored his fortunes twofold, blessing him with greater prosperity than before. Job received ten new children, a divine affirmation of his faithfulness. This remarkable turnaround came when Job interceded and prayed for the friends who had misjudged him, showing how compassion toward others opened the door to his own healing and blessing.

Job 42:10 (ESV)
'And the LORD restored the fortunes of Job, when he had prayed for his friends. And the LORD gave Job twice as much as he had before.'

JOB'S HISTORY IS RECORDED IN THE BOOK OF JOB.

Abraham

Abraham means "father of many nations."
His original name, Abram, means "exalted father."

Abraham was born in Ur of the Chaldeans. At 75, he responded to God's call to leave his homeland for an unknown land. This journey came with divine promises that he would become a great nation, receive God's blessing, and through him, all families on earth would be blessed.

Though wealthy in livestock, silver, and gold, Abraham lived as a nomad in Canaan. His faith faced many tests, most famously when God asked him to sacrifice his son Isaac. His trust in God's promises, even when they seemed impossible due to his and Sarah's old age, became a model of faith for generations to come.

Abraham showed leadership skills when he rescued his nephew Lot with 318 trained men. He displayed wisdom in his dealings with local kings and unusual generosity by refusing war spoils. His plea for Sodom and Gomorrah revealed his deep compassion for others.

Abraham died at the age of 175.

Twice, Abraham claimed his wife Sarah was merely his sister, putting her and others at risk. This revealed moments when fear overshadowed his trust in God's protection. His impatience led him to father Ishmael through Sarah's maidservant, Hagar, creating family conflicts that had far-reaching, generational consequences. Throughout his journey, Abraham struggled to fully trust God's timing and plan.

God confirmed that all nations would be blessed through Abraham and his descendants, making him a central figure in God's plan for human redemption. His trust in God was "counted to him as righteousness," establishing the foundation of faith-based righteousness. Abraham's willingness to sacrifice Isaac demonstrated complete trust in God, and foreshadowed God's later sacrifice of His own Son, Jesus Christ.

Genesis 12:11-13 (ESV)
'When he was about to enter Egypt, he said to Sarai his wife, "I know that you are a woman beautiful in appearance, and when the Egyptians see you, they will say, 'This is his wife.' Then they will kill me, but they will let you live. Say you are my sister, that it may go well with me because of you, and that my life may be spared for your sake." '

Genesis 15:5 (ESV)
'And he brought him outside and said, "Look toward heaven, and number the stars, if you are able to number them." Then he said to him, "So shall your offspring be." '

ABRAHAM'S HISTORY IS RECORDED IN GENESIS 11 TO 25.

Sarah

Sarah was initially named Sarai, meaning "princess."

Sarah was Abraham's wife and Isaac's mother. Her story begins when she left with Abraham in response to God's call to journey to an unknown land. Her extraordinary beauty created dangerous situations during their travels, causing both Pharaoh of Egypt and King Abimelech of Gerar to take her into their harems before God intervened.

Sarah endured the pain of childlessness in a culture where a woman's worth was largely measured by her ability to bear sons. For decades, she waited for God's promise of a son, even after she had stopped having monthly cycles. When divine visitors announced she would bear a son within a year, Sarah laughed behind the tent door in disbelief. Nevertheless, at 90 years old, she miraculously conceived and gave birth to Isaac, whose name means "laughter," reflecting both her initial skepticism and eventual joy.

Sarah lived to see Isaac grow into manhood and died at 127 years old in Hebron. Abraham mourned her deeply and purchased the cave of Machpelah as her burial place.

Sarah struggled with trusting God's timing. When the promised son didn't arrive, she took matters into her own hands by giving her Egyptian maidservant, Hagar, to Abraham as a surrogate. When Hagar conceived, Sarah was overcome with jealousy. She treated her maidservant so harshly that Hagar fled into the wilderness. Years later, Sarah laughed in disbelief at God's announcement of a son in her old age. Her actions created family division that extended through generations, with the descendants of Isaac and Ishmael developing into nations often in conflict with one another.

Genesis 16:6 (ESV)
'But Abram said to Sarai, "Behold, your servant is in your power; do to her as you please." Then Sarai dealt harshly with her, and she fled from her.'

God fulfilled His promise to Sarah by allowing her to conceive and bear a son long after her childbearing years had passed. The miracle of Isaac's birth transformed her skeptical laughter into joyful celebration. She declared, "God has brought me laughter, and everyone who hears about this will laugh with me." Despite her moments of doubt, Sarah is honored in Scripture as a woman of faith and an example of a godly woman. Through her son Isaac, Sarah became the matriarch of the covenant people and an ancestor of the Messiah. Her life demonstrates that God's promises prevail.

Hebrews 11:11 (ESV)
'By faith Sarah herself received power to conceive, even when she was past the age, since she considered him faithful who had promised.'

SARAH'S HISTORY IS RECORDED IN GENESIS 11 TO 23.

Hagar

Hagar means "flight" or "stranger."

Hagar was an Egyptian maidservant of Sarah, Abraham's wife. When Sarah remained childless, she gave Hagar to Abraham as a concubine to bear a child on her behalf, a common practice in those days.

After conceiving, Hagar began looking down on her mistress, which led Sarah to treat her harshly. Hagar fled into the wilderness, where an angel of the Lord found her by a spring. The angel instructed her to return and submit to Sarah, promising that her son Ishmael, conceived through Abraham, would become a "wild man" whose descendants would be too many to count.

Years later, after Sarah gave birth to Isaac, new tensions arose when Sarah saw Ishmael mocking her son. Sarah demanded that Abraham send Hagar and Ishmael away. Though troubled by this request, Abraham obeyed after God assured him that He would make a nation from Ishmael's descendants.

After conceiving Abraham's child, Hagar displayed pride and contempt toward Sarah. Her attitude worsened an already difficult situation and deepened the conflict within the household. By looking down on her mistress, Hagar showed a lack of understanding of her position and the proper relationships within the family structure of that time.

Genesis 16:4 (ESV)
'And he went in to Hagar, and she conceived. And when she saw that she had conceived, she looked with contempt on her mistress.'

Hagar is one of the few women in Scripture to whom God appeared personally and to whom He made direct promises. Cast into the wilderness, she faced watching her son die of thirst. God heard Ishmael's cry and provided a water well, saving her son's life and renewing His promise to make Ishmael a great nation. Despite her status as a foreign slave, Hagar experienced compassion from God, whom she named El-Roi, "the God who sees me." Her story reveals God's compassion for the vulnerable and His faithfulness to His promises regardless of social status or nationality.

Genesis 21:17-18 (ESV)
'And God heard the voice of the boy, and the angel of God called to Hagar from heaven and said to her, "What troubles you, Hagar? Fear not, for God has heard the voice of the boy where he is. Up! Lift up the boy, and hold him fast with your hand, for I will make him into a great nation."'

HAGAR'S ACCOUNT IS RECORDED IN GENESIS 16 AND 21.

Isaac

Isaac means "he will laugh" or "laughter."

Isaac was the child of promise, born to Abraham and Sarah in their old age. His birth brought much joy and amazement, as Sarah was 90 and Abraham was 100.

As a young man, Isaac demonstrated faith by allowing his father to bind him on the altar in obedience to God. Jewish tradition suggests he was 37 then, though the Bible does not specify his age. Unlike Abraham, who chose his own wife, Isaac's marriage to Rebekah was arranged through divine guidance.

Isaac became a prosperous farmer and herdsman. He reopened wells that the Philistines had filled and dug new ones. Rather than engaging in conflict, he often chose to avoid disputes.

Isaac lived for 180 years.

Isaac's favoritism toward Esau created a conflict that impacted his immediate family and future generations. Like his father, Isaac misrepresented his wife as his sister out of fear, showing a recurring pattern of deception.

Genesis 27:41 (ESV)
'Now Esau hated Jacob because of the blessing with which his father had blessed him, and Esau said to himself, "The days of mourning for my father are approaching; then I will kill my brother Jacob."'

God's covenant with Abraham continued through Isaac. He received divine blessings that affirmed God's promise to Abraham of a great nation. His peaceful nature and willingness to yield in disputes often reflected godly wisdom. His faithful near-sacrifice at Mount Moriah foreshadowed Christ's ultimate obedience to death.

Genesis 26:3 (ESV)
'Sojourn in this land, and I will be with you and will bless you, for to you and to your offspring I will give all these lands, and I will establish the oath that I swore to Abraham your father.'

ISAAC'S HISTORY IS RECORDED IN GENESIS 21 TO 35.

Rebekah

Rebekah means "to tie firmly" or "to bind."

After Sarah died, Abraham set out to find a wife for Isaac. He commanded his servant to travel to Aram Naharaim to select a bride from his family rather than a local Canaanite girl. As the servant stood by a water well with his men and camels, he prayed to God for guidance and asked the right woman to offer to water his camels. Rebekah fulfilled this sign precisely.

When asked to marry Isaac, Rebekah said, "I will go." She displayed courage in leaving her family for an unknown future. After meeting Isaac, she became his beloved wife and brought him comfort after his mother Sarah's death.

For twenty years, Rebekah remained childless until Isaac prayed for her. She then conceived twins, Esau and Jacob, who struggled within her womb. God revealed to her that "the older would serve the younger," giving her insight into their destinies.

Rebekah favored Jacob, her younger son. When Isaac intended to bless Esau, she devised a plan of deception, disguising Jacob as his brother to steal the blessing. This deception and her favoritism created a deep division in the family and fueled the bitter rivalry between her sons. It ultimately forced Jacob into exile and showed her unwillingness to trust God's timing to fulfill His promise without her interference.

Genesis 27:6-10 (ESV)
'Rebekah said to her son Jacob, "I heard your father speak to your brother Esau, 'Bring me game and prepare for me delicious food, that I may eat it and bless you before the Lord before I die.' Now therefore, my son, obey my voice as I command you. Go to the flock and bring me two good young goats, so that I may prepare from them delicious food for your father, such as he loves. And you shall bring it to your father to eat, so that he may bless you before he dies." '

Despite her flaws, Rebekah was crucial to God's covenant plan. Her departure from her homeland showed remarkable faith and courage, making her a fitting matriarch for God's people. She received a divine message about her sons that motivated her actions, though deceptive, and ensured that Jacob, the chosen son, received the covenant blessing, leading to the formation of Israel's twelve tribes and the lineage of the Messiah.

Genesis 25:23 (ESV)
'And the Lord said to her, "Two nations are in your womb, and two peoples from within you shall be divided; the one shall be stronger than the other, the older shall serve the younger." '

REBEKAH'S HISTORY IS RECORDED IN GENESIS 24 TO 28.

Jacob

Jacob means "supplanter" or "heel-grabber."
Israel means "one who strives with God" or "let God prevail."

Jacob was born grasping his twin brother Esau's heel. Jacob preferred a quieter life among the tents, unlike his rough and rugged brother. His early years were marked by trickery and manipulation, as he acquired his brother's birthright and blessing through clever deception.

Fleeing his brother's anger, Jacob spent 20 years working for his uncle Laban. During this time, he married Leah and Rachel, and fathered twelve sons and one daughter through them and their handmaids. The pivotal moment came when he wrestled with God at Peniel, receiving the new name Israel, meaning "one who strives with God."

In his later years, Jacob endured profound grief, believing his favorite son Joseph had died. This sorrow eventually turned to joy when he discovered Joseph was alive and ruling in Egypt. Jacob lived his final 17 years in Egypt under Joseph's care, where he delivered prophetic blessings to his sons and grandsons before dying at age 147.

Jacob tricked his father Isaac into giving him the blessing intended for Esau, causing deep family division with lasting consequences. His pattern of deception extended to his dealings with Laban and affected his relationships with his sons. Jacob's obvious favoritism toward Joseph created jealousy that nearly destroyed his family. His spiritual growth came slowly, requiring multiple divine encounters and difficult trials to shape his character. Rather than trusting God's promises, Jacob often relied on his own schemes, bringing unnecessary hardship and conflict upon himself.

Genesis 27:42 (ESV)
'But the words of Esau her older son were told to Rebekah. So she sent and called Jacob her younger son and said to him, "Behold, your brother Esau comforts himself about you by planning to kill you."'

God met Jacob in his struggle and gave him a new name, Israel. This marked a turning point in his life as he moved from self-reliance toward divine dependence, embracing God's plan for his life. The prophetic blessings Jacob gave his sons shaped the future of an entire nation. His life reveals God's patient work of transformation, molding a deceiver into a patriarch of faith.

Genesis 32:28 (ESV)
'Then he said, "Your name shall no longer be called Jacob, but Israel, for you have striven with God and with men, and have prevailed."'

JACOB'S HISTORY IS RECORDED IN GENESIS 25 TO 50.

Leah

Leah means "weary" or "delicate."

Leah was the older daughter of Laban and became Jacob's first wife through her father's deception. Scripture describes her as having "weak" or "delicate" eyes, contrasting her sister Rachel's beauty. After Jacob worked seven years to marry Rachel, Laban secretly substituted Leah on the wedding night, forcing Jacob to work another seven years for Rachel, whom he truly loved.

Though rejected by her husband, God blessed Leah with fertility while Rachel remained barren. She bore Jacob six sons, Reuben, Simeon, Levi, Judah, Issachar, Zebulun, and a daughter, Dinah. Leah's life was marked by the pain of being the unloved wife and the rivalry with her sister.

Unlike Rachel, who died in childbirth, Leah lived longer and was eventually buried with Jacob in the Cave of Machpelah, the family tomb where Abraham and Sarah were also buried. This final honor suggests that Jacob recognized her essential place in his life and in God's covenant plan.

Leah participated in Jacob's deception on his wedding night, likely under her father's direction. She lived with constant insecurity about her husband's rejection, repeatedly trying to earn his affection through bearing children. This insecurity created a competitive relationship with Rachel, contributing to family dysfunction. Her misplaced priorities showed her focus on seeking Jacob's approval rather than finding her worth in God.

Genesis 29:32 (ESV)
'And Leah conceived and bore a son, and she called his name Reuben, for she said, "Because the Lord has looked upon my affliction; for now my husband will love me."'

Leah was specifically noticed and blessed by God. Through her sons, she became the mother of half of Israel's tribes, including the priestly line through Levi and the royal Messianic line through Judah. As her childbearing continued, her focus shifted from seeking Jacob's approval to praising God, which is evident when she named her fourth son Judah, meaning "praise."
Though often overlooked, Leah's contribution to the covenant lineage was more significant than her beloved sister Rachel's, showing how God often works through those society marginalizes.

Genesis 29:35 (ESV)
'And she conceived again and bore a son, and said, "This time I will praise the Lord." Therefore she called his name Judah. Then she ceased bearing.'

LEAH'S HISTORY IS RECORDED IN GENESIS 29 TO 31.

Rachel

Rachel means "ewe" or "female sheep."

Rachel was the daughter of Laban and Jacob's beloved wife. Jacob sought refuge with his uncle Laban when he fled from his brother Esau. There, Jacob first encountered Rachel at a well where she was tending her father's sheep.

Scripture portrays Rachel as beautiful in form and appearance, and Jacob was immediately drawn to her. He agreed to work for Laban for seven years to win her hand in marriage. When the wedding day arrived, Laban deceived Jacob by substituting his older daughter, Leah. Jacob then worked another seven years to marry Rachel as well.

Rachel's life was marked by the pain of childlessness while watching her sister Leah bear multiple sons for Jacob. In her desperation, she gave her maidservant, Bilhah, to Jacob as a surrogate. Eventually, God answered Rachel's prayers, and she gave birth to Joseph.

During the family's journey back to Canaan, Rachel died while giving birth to her second son, Benjamin. She was buried near Bethlehem, and her tomb became a significant landmark in Israel's history.

Rachel struggled with intense jealousy toward her sister Leah, particularly regarding childbearing. This envy fueled a bitter rivalry between the sisters as they competed for Jacob's affection. In her desperate longing for sons, Rachel demanded of Jacob, "Give me children, or else I die!" revealing her impatience with God's timing. Rachel also stole her father's household idols when leaving his home, suggesting a lingering attachment to pagan practices despite her connection to the God of Abraham.

Genesis 30:1 (ESV)
'When Rachel saw that she bore Jacob no children, she envied her sister. She said to Jacob, "Give me children, or I shall die!" '

After years of heartbreaking infertility, God remembered Rachel and blessed her womb. She bore Joseph, who would become one of the most pivotal figures in Israel's history. Though Rachel died young, her sons, Joseph and Benjamin, became forefathers of influential tribes of Israel. Her deep longing for children was ultimately honored as she became known as a symbolic mother of Israel, whose memory endured through history.

Genesis 30:22-24 (ESV)
'Then God remembered Rachel, and God listened to her and opened her womb. She conceived and bore a son and said, "God has taken away my reproach." And she called his name Joseph, saying, "May the Lord add to me another son!" '

RACHEL'S HISTORY IS RECORDED IN GENESIS 29 TO 31.

Tamar

Tamar means "date palm" or "palm tree."

Tamar first appears in Scripture as the wife of Er, Judah's eldest son. After Er died because of his wickedness, Judah instructed his second son, Onan, to fulfill the levirate marriage duty by providing offspring for his deceased brother through Tamar. When Onan refused this responsibility and also died, Judah promised his third son, Shelah, to Tamar but failed to fulfill this pledge. This left Tamar in the difficult position of a childless widow with no inheritance rights or security.

Determined to secure her rightful place in the family line, Tamar disguised herself as a prostitute and positioned herself where Judah would pass by. Not recognizing his daughter-in-law, Judah slept with her, giving his signet, cord, and staff as a pledge for payment. Later, when Tamar's pregnancy was discovered, Judah prepared to have her executed until she produced these items, proving he was the father.

While Scripture does not explicitly condemn Tamar's deception, her methods reveal desperation that led to moral compromise. She resorted to trickery and sexual deception to secure justice, choosing to deceive Judah rather than wait for God's timing. Her actions, though born from legitimate grievances, involved pretending to be a prostitute and engaging in sexual relations with her father-in-law, behaviors prohibited under Mosaic law.

Genesis 38:14-15 (ESV)
'she took off her widow's garments and covered herself with a veil, wrapping herself up, and sat at the entrance to Enaim, which is on the road to Timnah. For she saw that Shelah was grown up, and she had not been given to him in marriage. When Judah saw her, he thought she was a prostitute, for she had covered her face.'

Despite the circumstances, God worked through Tamar's situation to continue the line that would eventually lead to King David and ultimately to Jesus Christ. She gave birth to twins Perez and Zerah, with Perez becoming a direct ancestor in the Messianic lineage. Tamar is one of only five women mentioned in Matthew's genealogy of Christ. Tamar received public vindication when Judah acknowledged his wrongdoing in withholding Shelah from her. This recognition restored her honor and secured her place in Judah's family.

Genesis 38:26 (ESV)
'Then Judah identified them and said, "She is more righteous than I, since I did not give her to my son Shelah." And he did not know her again.'

TAMAR'S ACCOUNT IS RECORDED IN GENESIS 38.

Joseph

Joseph means "He will add" or "God will add."

Joseph was Jacob's eleventh and favorite son, born to his beloved wife Rachel. As a young man, he received special treatment from his father, symbolized by a coat of many colors, which fueled his brothers' jealousy. His prophetic dreams suggesting his family would bow before him further strained these relationships.

At 17, Joseph was sold into slavery by his brothers after they initially plotted to kill him. Through exceptional management skills, he rose from slave to overseer in Potiphar's house. After being falsely accused and imprisoned, his God-given ability to interpret dreams eventually brought him before Pharaoh. His insightful interpretation and counsel led to his appointment as second-in-command in Egypt.

Through shrewd management during seven years of abundance followed by seven years of famine, Joseph saved Egypt and many surrounding nations. When reunited with his brothers, he showed remarkable forgiveness, recognizing God's purpose in his suffering. His life exemplified integrity, wisdom, and trust in God's providence, even amid the darkest circumstances.

Joseph died in Egypt at age 110.

The Bible does not record a significant moral failure in Joseph's life, as his character is portrayed as steadfast and obedient to God. In his youth, Joseph displayed some immaturity by sharing his dreams of greatness with his already jealous brothers. His challenges came primarily through external circumstances rather than personal sin.

Genesis 39:9 (ESV)
'He is not greater in this house than I am, nor has he kept back anything from me except you, because you are his wife. How then can I do this great wickedness and sin against God?'

God elevated Joseph to a position of authority in Egypt. Through this role, God transformed tragedy into triumph, saving countless lives when famine hit. Joseph's profound statement, "you meant evil against me, but God meant it for good," reveals a deep understanding of God's providence. Joseph's wise leadership preserved Egypt and the covenant family through whom the Messiah would come. His genuine forgiveness of his brothers showed exceptional spiritual maturity and broke the cycle of family dysfunction.

Genesis 41:56-57 (ESV)
'So when the famine had spread over all the land, Joseph opened all the storehouses and sold to the Egyptians, for the famine was severe in the land of Egypt. Moreover, all the earth came to Egypt to Joseph to buy grain, because the famine was severe over all the earth.'

JOSEPH'S HISTORY IS RECORDED IN GENESIS 30 TO 50.

Miriam

Miriam means "bitter" or "rebellious."

Miriam first appears in Scripture as the vigilant older sister watching over baby Moses as he floated in a basket on the River Nile. Her quick thinking led Moses to be raised by his own mother, though under the protection of Pharaoh's daughter. This early display of resourcefulness pointed to her future role as a leader of Israel.

As an adult, Miriam became the first woman in Scripture explicitly called a prophetess. After the Israelites crossed the Red Sea, she led the women in worship with tambourines, singing and dancing to celebrate God's victory over the Egyptian army.

Miriam held significant influence in Israel, alongside her brothers Moses and Aaron, who were leaders God sent to bring the people out of Egypt. Her guidance was especially important among the women during their wilderness journey. She formed part of the leadership trio God used, with Moses as lawgiver, Aaron as high priest, and Miriam as spiritual leader among the women.

Miriam died and was buried in the wilderness at Kadesh, not living to see the Promised Land.

Miriam challenged Moses' authority and God's choice of him as the primary leader of Israel, revealing her jealousy and pride. Her questioning of Moses' unique position showed discontent with her own role and a desire for greater recognition. This rebellion against God's established order brought divine judgment when she was struck with leprosy. This incident shows how even spiritual leaders can struggle with envy and ambition.

Despite her rebellion, God showed mercy to Miriam through Moses' prayers. Her leprosy was healed, and she rejoined the community after a period of discipline. Throughout Israel's history, she remained recognized as a leader God had sent to guide His people from Egypt. Her early protection of Moses preserved the life of Israel's future deliverer, playing a vital role in God's plan of redemption.

Numbers 12:1-2 (ESV)
'Miriam and Aaron spoke against Moses because of the Cushite woman whom he had married, for he had married a Cushite woman. And they said, "Has the LORD indeed spoken only through Moses? Has he not spoken through us also?" And the LORD heard it.'

Micah 6:4 (ESV)
'For I brought you up from the land of Egypt and redeemed you from the house of slavery, and I sent before you Moses, Aaron, and Miriam.'

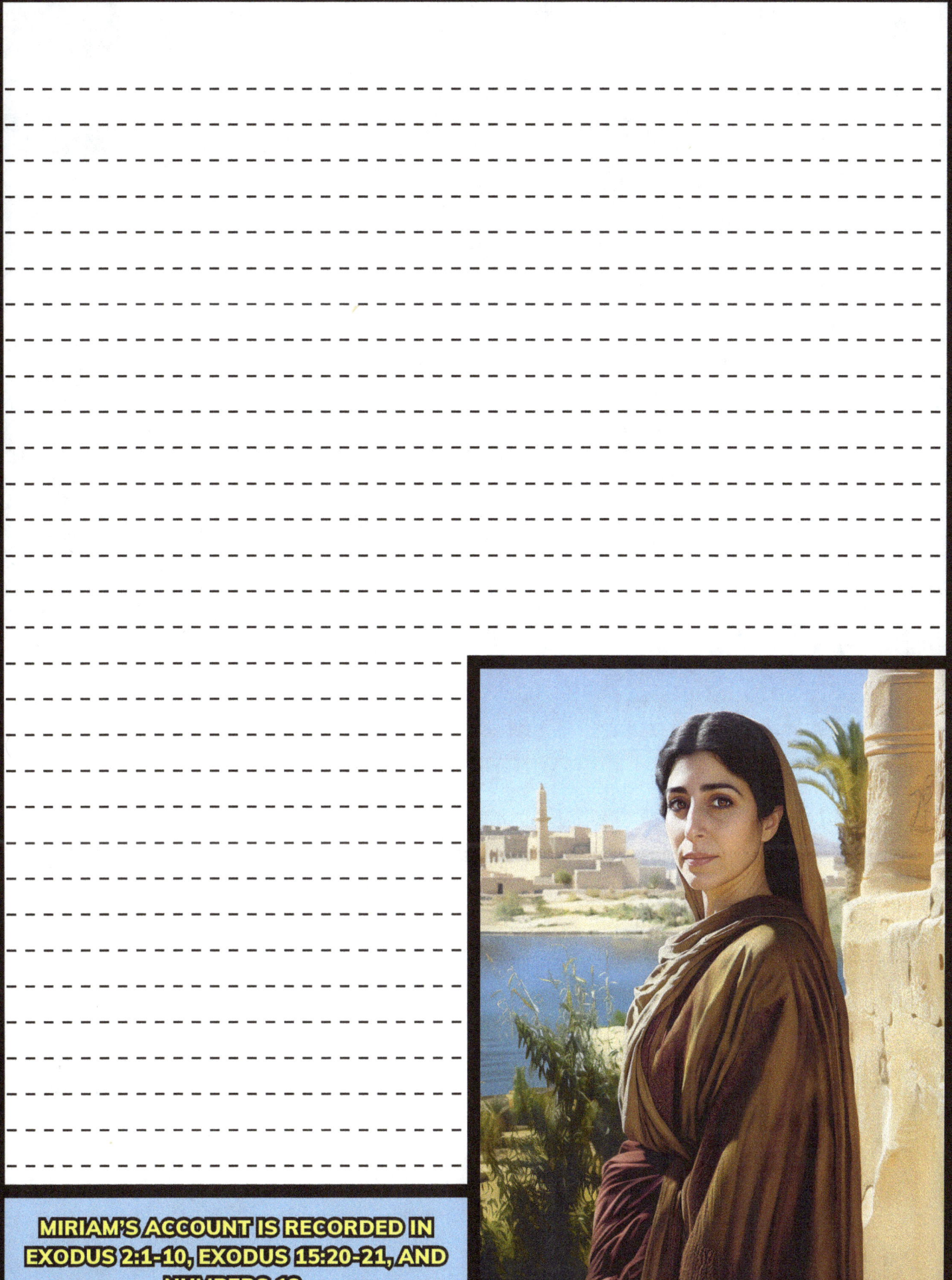

MIRIAM'S ACCOUNT IS RECORDED IN EXODUS 2:1-10, EXODUS 15:20-21, AND NUMBERS 12.

Moses

Moses means "drawn out" or "son" in Egyptian.

Moses was born at a time when Pharaoh ordered all Hebrew baby boys killed. His mother hid him for three months before placing him in a basket on the River Nile, where Pharaoh's daughter found and adopted him. He grew up in the Egyptian royal court, receiving a fine education.

After confronting and killing an Egyptian who beat a Hebrew slave, Moses fled to Midian where he lived as a shepherd for 40 years. There he married Zipporah, daughter of Jethro, and fathered two sons, Gershom and Eliezer. God appeared to him in a burning bush and called him to lead the Israelites from Egypt.

Despite his reluctance, and with his brother Aaron speaking for him, Moses confronted Pharaoh. With the help of God, he performed miraculous signs, and eventually led the Israelites out of Egypt. During the exodus, he parted the Red Sea, received the Ten Commandments, and guided the people through the wilderness for 40 years.

Though uniquely close to God, speaking with Him face to face, Moses could not enter the Promised Land because he disobeyed at Meribah. Before dying at age 120, Moses viewed Canaan from Mount Nebo but never entered.

Moses battled with self-doubt, repeatedly questioning God's choice of him as leader. At Meribah, he struck a rock in anger instead of speaking to it as God commanded. This act of disobedience cost him entry into the Promised Land. His temper flared at Meribah, and also earlier when he discovered Israel worshiping a golden calf, when he furiously shattered the stone tablets containing God's Law.

Numbers 20:11-12 (ESV)
'And Moses lifted up his hand and struck the rock with his staff twice, and water came out abundantly, and the congregation drank, and their livestock. And the LORD said to Moses and Aaron, "Because you did not believe in me, to uphold me as holy in the eyes of the people of Israel, therefore you shall not bring this assembly into the land that I have given them."'

God entrusted Moses with the Law and, despite his failures, kept him as Israel's leader until death. He enjoyed unmatched closeness with God, speaking with Him "face to face, as a man speaks to his friend", a privilege no other human experienced so fully. When God threatened to destroy Israel, Moses' prayers for mercy saved the people, showing his deep love for them. Later, Moses appeared with Elijah at the transfiguration of Jesus, confirming his lasting role in God's redemption plan.

Deuteronomy 34:10-12 (ESV)
'And there has not arisen a prophet since in Israel like Moses, whom the LORD knew face to face, none like him for all the signs and the wonders that the LORD sent him to do in the land of Egypt, to Pharaoh and to all his servants and to all his land, and for all the mighty power and all the great deeds of terror that Moses did in the sight of all Israel.'

MOSES'S HISTORY IS RECORDED IN EXODUS 2 TO 40.

Zipporah

Zipporah means "bird" or "sparrow."

Zipporah was the wife of Moses and the daughter of Jethro, a Midianite priest. She met Moses when he fled from Egypt after killing an Egyptian who was beating a Hebrew slave. When Moses helped Zipporah and her sisters water their flocks at a well, Jethro invited him to stay and eventually gave Zipporah to him in marriage. She bore Moses two sons, Gershom and Eliezer.

Zipporah is most notably remembered for her quick action that saved Moses' life when God sought to kill him on his way back to Egypt. Understanding the spiritual significance of the moment, she circumcised their son with a flint knife, touching Moses' feet with the foreskin, thereby fulfilling the covenant obligation Moses had neglected.

As a Midianite, Zipporah had cultural and religious differences from Moses, which created tension in their marriage. This cultural divide is evident in her reaction to circumcising her son, calling Moses a "bloody husband," suggesting her discomfort with Hebrew religious practices. Later, Moses sent Zipporah and their sons back to her father's house before the exodus from Egypt, indicating possible strain in their relationship during Moses' divine calling. This separation might reflect her reluctance to fully embrace Moses' mission or the challenges of supporting his prophetic role.

Exodus 18:2-3 (ESV)
'Now Jethro, Moses' father-in-law, had taken Zipporah, Moses' wife, after he had sent her home, along with her two sons. The name of the one was Gershom (for he said, "I have been a sojourner in a foreign land"),'

Despite the cultural differences and periods of separation, Zipporah demonstrated remarkable spiritual insight in a crucial moment. Her quick action to circumcise their son showed her understanding of covenant obligations, even when Moses neglected them. This decisive intervention saved Moses' life and enabled him to fulfill his divine mission to deliver Israel. The Bible records that Zipporah was reunited with Moses in the wilderness after the exodus. This reconciliation allowed her to witness the fulfillment of God's promises through Moses's leadership and see the deliverance of his people.

Exodus 18:5-6 (ESV)
'Jethro, Moses' father-in-law, came with his sons and his wife to Moses in the wilderness where he was encamped at the mountain of God. And when he sent word to Moses, "I, your father-in-law Jethro, am coming to you with your wife and her two sons with her," '

ZIPPORAH'S ACCOUNT IS RECORDED IN EXODUS 2:16-22, EXODUS 4:24-26, AND EXODUS 18:2-6.

Joshua

Joshua means "Yahweh is salvation" or "The LORD is salvation." His original name, Hosea, means "salvation," or "he will save."

Joshua first appears as Moses' aide and military commander, leading Israel's army against the Amalekites. He was one of the twelve spies sent to explore Canaan, and along with Caleb, he brought back an encouraging report, showing faith in God's promises. Moses changed his name from Hoshea to Joshua, reflecting his future role in God's plan.

As Moses's successor, Joshua received the spirit of wisdom through the laying on of Moses's hands. God personally commissioned him, promising to remain with him just as He had been with Moses. He led the Israelites across the Jordan River on dry ground, mirroring the earlier Red Sea crossing.

Under Joshua's leadership, Israel conquered much of Canaan, beginning with the miraculous fall of Jericho. He served as both military commander and spiritual leader, renewing Israel's covenant with God at Shechem. His memorable declaration, "As for me and my house, we will serve the LORD," stands as a powerful testament to his faithful leadership.

Before his death at 110 years old, he urged Israel to remain faithful to God and His covenant.

Joshua's leadership revealed moments of incomplete obedience. He failed to seek God's guidance before attacking the city of Ai, resulting in a devastating defeat for Israel. Joshua also did not fully drive out all the Canaanites from the Promised Land as commanded, which created lasting challenges for future generations. His leadership sometimes lacked the spiritual authority Moses had demonstrated, requiring God to intervene directly to guide His people.

Joshua 7:1 (ESV)
'But the people of Israel broke faith in regard to the devoted things, for Achan the son of Carmi, son of Zabdi, son of Zerah, of the tribe of Judah, took some of the devoted things. And the anger of the LORD burned against the people of Israel.'

Joshua walked in God's presence as he led the nation. The promise of victory and divine protection strengthened him throughout his journey, and he witnessed the fulfillment of God's promises firsthand. Joshua received divine strategies for victory, most notably at Jericho, proving God's faithfulness to guide those who trust Him. His steady leadership brought stability and hope to Israel during a period of great change.

Joshua 1:5 (ESV)
'No man shall be able to stand before you all the days of your life. Just as I was with Moses, so I will be with you. I will not leave you or forsake you.'

JOSHUA'S HISTORY IS RECORDED IN EXODUS 17:8-16, AND THE BOOK OF JOSHUA.

Rahab

Rahab means "wide" or "spacious." In the Hebrew Bible, it was also used to describe "pride" or "arrogance."

Rahab was a Canaanite woman living in Jericho when the Israelites prepared to conquer the Promised Land. Scripture identifies her as a prostitute, though some scholars suggest she may have been an innkeeper. She lived on the city wall, a strategic location vital to her involvement in the fall of Jericho.

When Joshua sent two spies to scout Jericho, they sought refuge in Rahab's house. After the king learned of their presence and demanded she surrender them, Rahab hid the men on her roof. She then misled the king's messengers, sending them away from the city on a false trail.

Rahab acted from her belief that Israel's God was "the God in heaven above and on earth below." This conviction led her to make a choice that would save her life and change her future.

By protecting the spies, Rahab secured a promise of safety for herself and her family during the coming attack on her city. She was told to hang a scarlet cord from her window as a marker. When Jericho fell, Joshua honored this agreement, sparing Rahab and her family while the rest of the city was destroyed.

Rahab lived as a prostitute in a pagan city, existing outside God's moral standards. Her work entangled her in the immoral customs of Canaanite society. When she protected the Israelite spies, she used deception, lying to Jericho's officials to save the men. Her actions came from her faith in Israel's God but still showed moral compromise.

Joshua 2:4-5 (ESV)
'But the woman had taken the two men and hidden them. And she said, "True, the men came to me, but I did not know where they were from. And when the gate was about to be closed at dark, the men went out. I do not know where the men went. Pursue them quickly, for you will overtake them." '

Rahab's trust in the God of Israel brought complete renewal to her life. When Jericho fell, she and her family were saved and welcomed into the Israelite community. Her marriage into the tribe of Judah placed her in the direct ancestry of King David and eventually Jesus Christ. Her path from Canaanite prostitute to ancestor of the Messiah stands as one of the most powerful stories of redemption in Scripture. The New Testament honors Rahab in the Hall of Faith as an example of saving faith, showing how God can take someone from society's edges and place them at the heart of His plan.

Hebrews 11:31 (ESV)
'By faith Rahab the prostitute did not perish with those who were disobedient, because she had given a friendly welcome to the spies.'

RAHAB'S ACCOUNT IS RECORDED IN JOSHUA 2, AND JOSHUA 6:17-25.

Deborah

Deborah means "bee" or "wasp."

Deborah served as both a prophetess and judge during the time when Jabin, king of Canaan, oppressed the Israelites. She stands out as the only female judge mentioned in the Bible and one of the few women described as a prophetess.

Known for her wisdom and authority, Deborah held court under a palm tree between Ramah and Bethel in the hill country of Ephraim. When God directed her to address Israel's oppression, she called Barak from Naphtali and told him God's command to lead 10,000 men against Sisera. Barak responded with evident respect for her authority yet showed hesitation about the task: "If you go with me, I will go; but if you don't go with me, I won't go." Deborah agreed but told him the honor of victory would go to a woman. This came true when Jael, wife of Heber the Kenite, killed Sisera by driving a tent peg through his temple as he slept.

As judge, prophetess, and military advisor, Deborah is one of the most remarkable leaders in Israel's history. She blended divine guidance with practical wisdom and courage, inspiring others to act faithfully during times of crisis.

The Bible does not point out specific moral failures in Deborah's life, yet she led during a time of widespread spiritual compromise in Israel. Her need to urge Barak to fulfill his calling shows she faced resistance and likely struggled with limited authority in a male-dominated society.

God raised Deborah as a leader at a crucial moment in Israel's history, working through her to bring freedom and peace. Her leadership mixed prophetic insight, wise judgment, and battle strategy, showing how God equips those He chooses. Under her guidance, Israel enjoyed forty years of peace, one of the longest stable periods in the book of Judges. Her step into leadership when men hesitated, reveals how God works through unexpected people to fulfill His plan.

Judges 4:8 (ESV)
'Barak said to her, "If you will go with me, I will go, but if you will not go with me, I will not go." '

Judges 5:31 (ESV)
' "So may all your enemies perish, O LORD! But your friends be like the sun as he rises in his might." And the land had rest for forty years.'

DEBORAH'S ACCOUNT IS RECORDED IN JUDGES 4 AND 5.

Gideon

Gideon means "feller" or "one who cuts down."

Gideon lived during a time when Israel suffered under Midianite oppression so severe that Israelites hid in mountains and caves. When the angel of the Lord found him, he was threshing wheat in a winepress to conceal it from raiders. Though he came from the weakest clan in Manasseh and was the least in his family, God chose him to deliver Israel.

Before accepting this calling, Gideon requested confirmation through several signs, including the well-known fleece tests. His first act of faith came when he destroyed his father's altar to Baal and the Asherah pole beside it. This bold move earned him the name Jerubbaal, meaning "let Baal contend against him."

God reduced Gideon's army from 32,000 to just 300 men to show that victory would come from divine power, not human strength. Armed with trumpets, empty jars, and torches, Gideon led this small band to defeat the vast Midianite forces. Following this victory, Israel enjoyed forty years of peace under his leadership. Gideon lived to an old age before his death.

When first called by God, Gideon responded with fear and doubt. This reluctance revealed his struggle with self-confidence when faced with God's assignment. After defeating the Midianites, Gideon created a golden ephod that became a spiritual trap for him and his family, ultimately leading Israel toward idolatry. Though he verbally refused kingship, his actions told a different story. He took many wives and named his son Abimelech, meaning "my father is king." Despite his military success, Gideon failed to establish lasting spiritual reform, and Israel returned to idol worship after his death.

Judges 6:15 (ESV)
'And he said to him, "Please, Lord, how can I save Israel? Behold, my clan is the weakest in Manasseh, and I am the least in my father's house." '

Gideon's small band of fighting men overcame overwhelming odds. His story shows how divine strength conquers fear and how God patiently works through human weakness. Scripture honors Gideon as a hero of faith despite his shortcomings, revealing God's gracious assessment of His servants. God's victory with just 300 men established a pattern repeated throughout Scripture, using only a few to fulfill His divine plans.

Judges 7:7 (ESV)
'And the LORD said to Gideon, "With the 300 men who lapped I will save you and give the Midianites into your hand, and let all the others go every man to his home." '

GIDEON'S ACCOUNT IS RECORDED IN JUDGES 6 TO 8.

Ruth

Ruth means "friend" or "companion."

Ruth was a Moabite woman who married into an Israelite family that had moved to Moab during a famine in Judah. After her husband, father-in-law, and brother-in-law died, Ruth chose to stay with her mother-in-law Naomi rather than return to her own people.

Her famous words to Naomi, "Where you go I will go, and where you stay I will stay. Your people will be my people and your God my God," showed remarkable loyalty and faith. Ruth followed Naomi back to Bethlehem, where she supported them both by gathering leftover grain in the fields of Boaz, a wealthy relative of Naomi's husband.

Boaz noticed Ruth's kindness to Naomi and her hard work. Following Naomi's advice, Ruth approached Boaz at the threshing floor and requested marriage according to custom. Boaz married Ruth, and their son Obed became the grandfather of King David, placing Ruth in the family line of Jesus despite being a foreigner.

Ruth is one of only five women named directly in Matthew's genealogy of Jesus.

Ruth faced many barriers that made her life very hard. As a foreigner from Moab, a traditional enemy of Israel, a childless widow, and an immigrant, she was vulnerable in every way. Though the Bible doesn't point out personal failings, Ruth's situation shows how circumstances beyond one's control can create overwhelming challenges.

God turned Ruth's faithfulness into a legacy that lasted for generations. From complete poverty, she found a place in Israel's community and security through her marriage to Boaz. Most importantly, she became the great-grandmother of King David and part of the family line that led to Jesus, showing God's care for outsiders and His plan to include non-Israelites in His salvation story.

Ruth 1:3-5 (ESV)
'But Elimelech, the husband of Naomi, died, and she was left with her two sons. These took Moabite wives; the name of the one was Orpah and the name of the other Ruth. They lived there about ten years, and both Mahlon and Chilion died, so that the woman was left without her two sons and her husband.'

Ruth 4:13-14 (ESV)
'So Boaz took Ruth, and she became his wife. And he went in to her, and the LORD gave her conception, and she bore a son. Then the women said to Naomi, "Blessed be the LORD, who has not left you this day without a redeemer, and may his name be renowned in Israel!" '

RUTH'S HISTORY IS RECORDED IN THE BOOK OF RUTH.

Naomi

Naomi means "pleasant" or "lovely."

Naomi was an Israelite woman from Bethlehem who fled to Moab with her husband Elimelech and their two sons during a severe famine in Judah. Tragedy struck in this foreign land when her husband died, leaving her a widow in a strange country. Her sons married local Moabite women, Orpah and Ruth, but after about ten years, both sons also died, leaving all three women widowed and vulnerable.

When news reached Naomi that the famine in Judah had ended, she resolved to return to her homeland. Both daughters-in-law began the journey with her, but after Naomi's insistence they return to their families, Orpah reluctantly turned back. Ruth, however, pledged unfailing loyalty to Naomi and her God.

In Bethlehem, Naomi shrewdly guided Ruth toward Boaz, a close relative who could act as their kinsman-redeemer. This relationship led to marriage between Ruth and Boaz, and when they had a son named Obed, Naomi embraced her role as grandmother to the boy who would become the grandfather of King David.

Naomi's spirit crumbled under the weight of her losses, and bitter grief clouded her view of God's providence. She openly blamed God for her misfortunes and urged her daughters-in-law to leave her and return to their Moabite gods, potentially denying them knowledge of the true God. Her narrow focus on personal suffering blinded her to God's ongoing care. Upon returning to Bethlehem, she told the townspeople to call her Mara instead, as she blamed God for her bitterness.

Despite Naomi's crushing losses, God provided Ruth as her loyal companion when she most needed support. Through Ruth's marriage to Boaz, Naomi gained material security and a grandson who restored her standing in the community. The women of Bethlehem rejoiced with her as she cared for Obed, a child who would continue her family line and become an ancestor of King David and, eventually, Jesus Christ. Her journey demonstrates how God works through human suffering to bring restoration and blessing.

Ruth 1:20-21 (ESV)
'She said to them, "Do not call me Naomi; call me Mara, for the Almighty has dealt very bitterly with me. I went away full, and the LORD has brought me back empty. Why call me Naomi, when the LORD has testified against me and the Almighty has brought calamity upon me?" '

Ruth 4:14-15 (ESV)
'Then the women said to Naomi, "Blessed be the LORD, who has not left you this day without a redeemer, and may his name be renowned in Israel! He shall be to you a restorer of life and a nourisher of your old age, for your daughter-in-law who loves you, who is more to you than seven sons, has given birth to him." '

NAOMI'S HISTORY IS RECORDED IN THE BOOK OF RUTH.

Samson

Samson means "child of the sun" or "little sun."

Samson was born after an angel announced his arrival to his previously barren mother. His parents, Manoah and his wife, received specific directions about his upbringing, that he would be a Nazirite from birth, marking him as specially consecrated to God. This meant that he could not drink wine, cut his hair, or touch dead bodies.

Gifted with supernatural strength, Samson performed remarkable feats. He killed a lion with his bare hands, captured 300 foxes to burn Philistine fields, and defeated 1,000 men using only a donkey's jawbone. Despite his power, his weakness for Philistine women eventually led to his downfall.

He served as a judge of Israel for twenty years during Philistine oppression. Though often driven by personal vengeance rather than national leadership, God used his actions to begin freeing Israel from Philistine control. His final act of pulling down the temple of Dagon killed more enemies than he had during his lifetime, though it cost him his own life.

Samson repeatedly broke his Nazirite vow through contact with dead bodies, likely drinking wine, and revealing the secret of his strength to Delilah. He wasted his divine gifts through pride and self-indulgence, lacking control over his sexual impulses and anger. His poor choices led to his capture by the Philistines. His disobedience brought about his blindness, imprisonment, and ultimately, death.

Judges 16:21 (ESV)
'And the Philistines seized him and gouged out his eyes and brought him down to Gaza and bound him with bronze shackles. And he ground at the mill in the prison.'

Samson's final prayer revealed genuine dependence on God, marking a spiritual turning point. In his last moments, God restored his strength one final time. This enabled him to defeat many enemies and bring judgment to those who had oppressed Israel. Samson's story shows how God works through human weakness and failure to fulfill His divine purposes.

Judges 16:30 (ESV)
'And Samson said, "Let me die with the Philistines." Then he bowed with all his strength, and the house fell upon the lords and upon all the people who were in it. So the dead whom he killed at his death were more than those whom he had killed during his life.'

SAMSON'S ACCOUNT IS RECORDED IN JUDGES 13 TO 16.

Hannah

Hannah means "favor" or "grace."

Hannah was one of two wives of Elkanah, a Levite from the hill country of Ephraim. While Elkanah's other wife Peninnah had children, Hannah remained childless, a condition viewed as shameful in ancient Israel. Each year when they traveled to worship at Shiloh, Peninnah would taunt Hannah about her barrenness, causing her great distress.

During one such visit, Hannah was so grieved that she wept and refused to eat. She went to the tabernacle alone and prayed silently with such emotion that her lips moved without sound. Hannah vowed that if God granted her a son, she would dedicate him to the Lord's service for life. Eli, the high priest, initially misjudged her for being drunk, but then saw her distress and blessed her prayer.

God answered Hannah, and she bore a son named Samuel, which means "heard by God." True to her promise, Hannah brought young Samuel to serve under Eli at the Tabernacle once he was weaned. Hannah's influence shaped Israel's history through her son Samuel, who became a pivotal prophet and judge. Her sacrifice demonstrates remarkable faith and devotion.

Hannah's deep longing for a child consumed her with grief and anguish. Her bitter tears and emotional response to Peninnah's taunts reveal her struggle to find peace amid her sorrow. When praying for a son, she struck what seemed like a bargain with God, promising to dedicate her child to lifelong service if her prayer was granted. This suggested she viewed her relationship with God as somewhat transactional rather than trusting His wisdom unconditionally.

1 Samuel 1:10 (ESV)
'She was deeply distressed and prayed to the Lord and wept bitterly.'

God answered Hannah's prayer and worked through her son to bring spiritual renewal to all of Israel. Samuel became one of Israel's most significant prophets and judges, bridging the period between Judges and Kings. After fulfilling her vow, Hannah was blessed with three more sons and two daughters, transforming her barrenness into abundance. The prayer she offered in thanksgiving profoundly expresses God's sovereignty and care for those society overlooks.

1 Samuel 2:1 (ESV)
'And Hannah prayed and said, "My heart exults in the Lord ; my horn is exalted in the Lord . My mouth derides my enemies, because I rejoice in your salvation." '

HANNAH'S ACCOUNT IS RECORDED IN
1 SAMUEL 1 AND 2.

Samuel

Samuel means "God has heard" or "name of God."

Samuel was born to Hannah in answer to her fervent prayer. From childhood, she dedicated him to God's service. As a young boy serving under Eli, the priest at Shiloh, he received his first prophetic call when God spoke to him about judgment coming upon Eli's house.

He grew to be recognized throughout Israel as a trustworthy prophet of the Lord, and "none of his words fell to the ground." He established a circuit court, traveling regularly between Bethel, Gilgal, Mizpah, and Ramah to judge Israel. Under his leadership, Israel experienced a significant spiritual revival, turning from Baal and Ashtaroth to serve the Lord alone.

When the people demanded a king, Samuel initially resisted, seeing it as rejection of God's direct rule. Yet, following divine guidance, he anointed both Saul and later David as kings over Israel. He served as prophet and advisor throughout his life, speaking truth to power, as shown in his bold confrontation with Saul over disobedience.

Samuel appointed his two sons as judges over Israel. These sons, unlike their father, took bribes and perverted justice. Their corruption prompted the elders to ask Samuel for a king to rule them like other nations had. Samuel struggled with this request, seeing it as rejection of his leadership and God's kingship over Israel. His initial resistance revealed his difficulty accepting the new type of governance God had in mind for Israel.

1 Samuel 8:4-6 (ESV)
'Then all the elders of Israel gathered together and came to Samuel at Ramah and said to him, "Behold, you are old and your sons do not walk in your ways. Now appoint for us a king to judge us like all the nations." But the thing displeased Samuel when they said, "Give us a king to judge us." And Samuel prayed to the LORD.'

Despite the shift to monarchy, God worked powerfully through Samuel. His prophetic voice remained respected, and God confirmed his leadership. Samuel gathered and taught many prophets, ensuring prophetic ministry continued in Israel for generations. His faithful life shows unwavering commitment to God's purposes. Even after death, his legacy endured through his anointing of David, under whom Israel reached its golden age.

1 Samuel 12:24 (ESV)
'Only fear the LORD and serve him faithfully with all your heart. For consider what great things he has done for you.'

SAMUEL'S HISTORY IS RECORDED IN 1 SAMUEL 2 TO 25.

David

David means "beloved" or "beloved one."

David grew up as the youngest of Jesse's eight sons, tending sheep in the hills of Bethlehem. While still young, the prophet Samuel secretly anointed him as Israel's future king. His years as a shepherd built both his courage in fighting predators and his musical talent, which later filled the Psalms.

He defeated the giant Philistine warrior Goliath using only a sling and stone. This victory led to service in King Saul's court, where he formed a deep friendship with Saul's son Jonathan. As Saul grew increasingly jealous, David spent years as a fugitive in the wilderness.

After Saul's death, David ruled Judah, then united all twelve tribes under his leadership. He captured Jerusalem, establishing it as his capital city. Under his rule, Israel expanded its borders and grew into a regional power. Though he committed grave sins, his adultery with Bathsheba and arranging her husband Uriah's death, David's genuine repentance and devotion to God earned him the title "a man after God's own heart."

He died at age 70, leaving behind a powerful kingdom and lasting legacy.

David's darkest moment came when he took Bathsheba for himself and arranged her husband's death in battle. This betrayal violated multiple commandments and marked the most significant moral failure of his life. The consequences of these sins affected his family and kingdom for years afterward. David also failed as a father, unable to address the assault of his daughter Tamar by her half-brother Amnon, and the violent revenge taken by his son Absalom.

God forgave David and renewed his spirit after David poured out his heart in genuine repentance. God promised that David's royal line would continue forever, ultimately fulfilled in Jesus Christ, the Son of David. David remains the only person in Scripture called "a man after God's own heart," revealing God's delight in those who passionately pursue relationship with Him. The Psalms David wrote continue to guide believers in worship, prayer, and spiritual growth today. His story reminds us that true repentance opens the door to restoration with God.

2 Samuel 11:4 (ESV)
'So David sent messengers and took her, and she came to him, and he lay with her. (Now she had been purifying herself from her uncleanness.) Then she returned to her house.'

2 Samuel 7:16 (ESV)
'And your house and your kingdom shall be made sure forever before me. Your throne shall be established forever.'

DAVID'S HISTORY IS RECORDED IN 1 SAMUEL 16 TO 31, 2 SAMUEL, AND 1 KINGS 1 TO 2:11.

Abigail

Abigail means "my father's joy" or "father's joy."

Abigail, a wise and beautiful woman, was married to Nabal, a wealthy but foolish man. When David, while fleeing from King Saul, requested provisions from Nabal after protecting his shepherds and flocks, Nabal responded with insults and refused. This prompted David to gather armed men to attack Nabal's household.

Learning of this danger, Abigail quickly gathered provisions and rode out to meet David without informing her husband. Upon meeting David, she bowed before him and delivered one of Scripture's most diplomatic speeches. She acknowledged her husband's foolishness, prevented David from bloodshed that would have stained his future kingship, and spoke prophetically about God's plan to establish David's dynasty.

After returning home, Abigail told Nabal what had happened. Hearing her account, his heart failed him, becoming like stone. Ten days later, he died. When David learned of Nabal's death, he sent for Abigail to become his wife. She later bore David a son named Chileab, also called Daniel.

Abigail endured a difficult marriage to Nabal, a harsh and mean-spirited man. She acted independently in a culture where such behavior from wives was rarely accepted, potentially undermining her marital relationship despite her noble intentions. Though her actions saved lives, some might view her conduct as disloyal to her husband's authority.

Abigail's wisdom and diplomatic skills saved many lives and prevented David from committing a sin that would have damaged his future reign. Her prophetic understanding of God's plan for David showed remarkable spiritual insight. After Nabal's death ended her troubled marriage, she became the wife of David, Israel's future king, a position that recognized her wisdom and character. Her quick thinking and brave action during crisis revealed how God uses a person's natural gifts at crucial moments to fulfill His purposes.

1 Samuel 25:18-19 (ESV)
'Then Abigail made haste and took two hundred loaves and two skins of wine and five sheep already prepared and five seahs of parched grain and a hundred clusters of raisins and two hundred cakes of figs, and laid them on donkeys. And she said to her young men, "Go on before me; behold, I come after you." But she did not tell her husband Nabal.'

1 Samuel 25:32-33 (ESV)
'And David said to Abigail, "Blessed be the LORD, the God of Israel, who sent you this day to meet me! Blessed be your discretion, and blessed be you, who have kept me this day from bloodguilt and from working salvation with my own hand!"'

ABIGAIL'S ACCOUNT IS RECORDED IN 1 SAMUEL 25.

Solomon

Solomon means "peace" or "peaceful one."

Solomon was the son of David and Bathsheba. God chose him to succeed David as king. Before taking the throne, he received special instruction from his father about building the temple.

When Solomon began his reign, God appeared to him in a dream and offered him anything he desired. Solomon asked for wisdom to govern well, which pleased God so much that He gave him unmatched wisdom along with wealth and honor. His wisdom became legendary, drawing visitors from distant lands, including the Queen of Sheba.

Under Solomon's leadership, Israel reached its greatest size and economic prosperity. He completed massive building projects, including Jerusalem's magnificent temple and his own palace. He demonstrated profound knowledge of nature, writing 3,000 proverbs and 1,005 songs. Despite these achievements, his many foreign marriages eventually pulled his heart away from God.

Solomon turned from God by gathering excessive wealth and horses, directly violating the laws for Israel's kings. His many foreign wives led him into idolatry. He burdened Israel with heavy taxes and forced labor, creating problems that eventually split the kingdom. Despite his extraordinary wisdom, his poor choices divided the nation and cost him God's favor. His spiritual decline happened gradually, showing how small compromises can slowly weaken our devotion to God over time.

1 Kings 11:4 (ESV)
'For when Solomon was old his wives turned away his heart after other gods, and his heart was not wholly true to the LORD his God, as was the heart of David his father.'

Early in his reign, God blessed Solomon with wisdom to rule justly. This wisdom brought peace and prosperity to Israel. His gift reminds us how God rewards obedience. Solomon's temple became the center of worship and a dwelling place for God's presence among His people. The wisdom books he wrote, Proverbs, Ecclesiastes, and Song of Songs, continue to offer spiritual and practical guidance for believers throughout history.

1 Kings 3:9 (ESV)
'Give your servant therefore an understanding mind to govern your people, that I may discern between good and evil, for who is able to govern this your great people?'

SOLOMON'S HISTORY IS RECORDED IN 2 SAMUEL 12:24-25, 1 KINGS 1 TO 11, AND 2 CHRONICLES 1 TO 9.

Elijah

Elijah means "my God is Yahweh" or "the LORD is my God."

Elijah, the Tishbite, is first mentioned in the Bible announcing a drought to King Ahab. During this time, God provided for him through ravens by the Brook Cherith and later through a widow at Zarephath, whose son he restored to life.

His defining moment came when he confronted Baal's prophets on Mount Carmel. There, he challenged them to prove which god was real. When fire from heaven consumed Elijah's water-soaked sacrifice, it sparked revival throughout Israel. Despite this victory, he soon fell into despair and fled from Queen Jezebel's threats. God met and renewed him at Mount Horeb.

Throughout his ministry, Elijah boldly spoke truth to power, confronting King Ahab over Naboth's vineyard. He mentored Elisha as his successor and, remarkably, was taken to heaven in a whirlwind with fiery chariots and horses. His legacy was so profound that Jewish tradition awaited his return before the Messiah's coming.

Elijah struggled with deep despair after fleeing his enemies. He once begged God to take his life rather than continue his difficult mission. These moments of weakness revealed his human frailty, often requiring God's intervention and restoration before he could resume his work. His claim, "I alone am left," showed a narrowed perspective that God corrected by revealing 7,000 faithful Israelites. Even following his greatest triumph at Mount Carmel, Elijah's fear of Jezebel drove him into the wilderness, showing how spiritual victories can quickly give way to emotional valleys.

1 Kings 19:4 (ESV)
'But he himself went a day's journey into the wilderness and came and sat down under a broom tree. And he asked that he might die, saying, "It is enough; now, O LORD, take away my life, for I am no better than my fathers." '

God restored Elijah through a gentle whisper at Mount Horeb. This encounter renewed his purpose and strength, while God's faithful presence sustained his ministry. His showdown with Baal's prophets remains one of Scripture's most powerful demonstrations of God's omnipotence. Unique among prophets, Elijah was taken to heaven without experiencing death, foreshadowing Christ's ascension and believers' future transformation. His appearance at Jesus' Transfiguration confirmed his enduring importance in God's redemptive plan and the connection between the old and new covenants.

1 Kings 19:13 (ESV)
'And when Elijah heard it, he wrapped his face in his cloak and went out and stood at the entrance of the cave. And behold, there came a voice to him and said, "What are you doing here, Elijah?" '

ELIJAH'S HISTORY IS RECORDED IN 1 KINGS 17 TO 19, 1 KINGS 21, AND 2 KINGS 1 AND 2.

Hosea

Hosea means "salvation" or "he will save."

Hosea prophesied during a time when Israel enjoyed prosperity that masked deep spiritual decay. God commanded him to marry Gomer, a woman who would prove unfaithful, creating a living illustration of Israel's unfaithfulness to God. Through this painful personal experience, Hosea learned firsthand about God's persistent love for His wayward people.

When Gomer abandoned him for other lovers, God instructed Hosea to redeem her and restore her as his wife. This act symbolized God's commitment to redeem Israel despite their spiritual adultery. Hosea's ministry spanned the final years of the northern kingdom of Israel, as he warned them of coming judgment while promising future restoration.

Hosea blended strong words of judgment with tender expressions of God's love. He portrayed God as a loving husband and a caring parent, revealing the depth of Israel's betrayal and the persistence of divine love. His personal story became a powerful metaphor illustrating God's faithful love despite human unfaithfulness.

Hosea endured pain and public humiliation through his marriage to unfaithful Gomer. Loving a spouse who repeatedly betrayed him tested Hosea's emotional strength and spiritual resolve. The brokenness in his marriage symbolized Israel's more profound spiritual condition as his personal suffering mirrored the nation's betrayal of God. Hosea's difficult experiences became inseparable from his prophetic calling, revealing the personal cost of obeying God's unconventional commands.

Hosea's life became a living parable of God's relentless love, offering Scripture one of its most powerful images of divine faithfulness, as God promised to heal broken relationships with His people. Hosea's story demonstrates the possibility of renewal even after profound betrayal, and his prophecy concludes with promises of restoration extending beyond Israel, including healing for the land itself. Hosea's message shaped later prophetic writings and influenced New Testament understanding of God's covenant love fulfilled through Christ.

Hosea 1:6 (ESV)
'She conceived again and bore a daughter. And the Lord said to him, "Call her name No Mercy, for I will no more have mercy on the house of Israel, to forgive them at all."'

Hosea 14:4 (ESV)
'I will heal their apostasy; I will love them freely, for my anger has turned from them.'

HOSEA'S PROPHESIES ARE CONTAINED IN THE BOOK OF HOSEA.

Isaiah means "salvation of the LORD" or "the LORD is salvation."

Isaiah began his prophetic ministry the year King Uzziah died, when he witnessed a dramatic vision of God's holiness in the temple. According to Jewish tradition, he was related to the royal family, which granted him direct access to kings. He served as an advisor during the reigns of Uzziah, Jotham, Ahaz, and Hezekiah.

His ministry lasted about 40 years during a significant period in Judah's history. He confronted the looming threat of the Assyrian Empire and guided kings through political crises. When King Hezekiah fell deathly ill, Isaiah delivered God's message of healing, confirming it with the miraculous sign of the sun's shadow moving backward.

Isaiah's prophecies addressed both present situations and future events. He provided remarkably detailed prophecies about the coming Messiah, including His virgin birth, suffering, and future kingdom. His writings contain powerful poetic descriptions of God's character and promises of restoration.

Jewish tradition holds that he was martyred during King Manasseh's reign.

Isaiah often expressed deep sorrow over the people's sins. His laments revealed the heavy burden he carried ministering to them and his acute awareness of God's holiness. Throughout his ministry, Isaiah faced rejection from the very people and leaders he was called to address. His prophetic duty required him to keep speaking God's truth even when he knew his audience wasn't listening, putting his perseverance and faith to the test.

Isaiah 6:5 (ESV)
'And I said: "Woe is me! For I am lost; for I am a man of unclean lips, and I dwell in the midst of a people of unclean lips; for my eyes have seen the King, the LORD of hosts!" '

God validated Isaiah's ministry through revelations of hope and future restoration. His writings offer promises of comfort and renewal that inspire seekers of God's truth. Isaiah received exceptionally detailed Messianic prophecies, foreseeing Christ's virgin birth, suffering, and ultimate glory. The symbolic purification of his lips with coal demonstrated God's provision for human inadequacy and prepared him for his prophetic calling.

Isaiah 40:31 (ESV)
'but they who wait for the Lord shall renew their strength; they shall mount up with wings like eagles; they shall run and not be weary; they shall walk and not faint.'

ISAIAH'S PROPHESIES ARE CONTAINED IN THE BOOK OF ISAIAH.

Jeremiah

Jeremiah means "Yahweh will raise" or "Yahweh will exalt."

Jeremiah was called to be a prophet while still young, during the reign of King Josiah. Known as the "weeping prophet," he served during Judah's darkest period, witnessing Jerusalem's destruction and the exile to Babylon. God instructed him not to marry or have children because of the coming judgment.

His ministry faced fierce opposition. He endured beatings, public humiliation in stocks, near-death in a muddy cistern, and multiple imprisonments. He faithfully delivered God's messages of judgment and restoration through rejection and persecution.

After Jerusalem fell, Jeremiah was forced to Egypt with a group of survivors, though he had warned against this path. He authored Lamentations, grieving Jerusalem's destruction. During his forty-year ministry, he kept detailed records through his scribe Baruch, even rewriting everything after King Jehoiakim burned the first scroll. Though his prophecies of judgment came true in his lifetime, he also proclaimed God's promise of a new covenant with His people.

Jeremiah battled profound sorrow over the people's sins. His words often revealed an unbearable burden, questioning God when he saw the wicked prosper. The prophet endured crushing loneliness, forbidden by God from marriage and normal community life. In his darkest moment, he accused God of deceiving him and contemplated abandoning his calling altogether. His raw human pain stands honestly recorded alongside his faithful service.

Jeremiah 20:14 (ESV)
'Cursed be the day on which I was born! The day when my mother bore me, let it not be blessed!'

Jeremiah's life was shaped by divine purpose, called and set apart by God before his birth. The Lord affirmed his ministry through the promise of a new covenant, offering hope beyond the old covenant's failure and ultimately fulfilled in Christ. His message pointed to a future restoration for God's people. Jeremiah's story reveals how God's promises sustain even those who bear deep sorrow. Though facing constant rejection, persecution, and few visible results, his faithfulness amid suffering exemplifies steadfast perseverance in serving God.

Jeremiah 31:31 (ESV)
'Behold, the days are coming, declares the LORD, when I will make a new covenant with the house of Israel and the house of Judah,'

JEREMIAH'S PROPHESIES ARE CONTAINED IN THE BOOK OF JEREMIAH AND THE BOOK OF LAMENTATIONS.

Daniel

Daniel means "God is my judge."

Daniel was taken to Babylon as a young man during the first deportation from Jerusalem. Together with his three friends, he refused the king's food, showing his devotion to God even in a foreign land. His remarkable wisdom and ability to interpret dreams earned him a prominent position in the Babylonian court.

Daniel served under several kings, including Nebuchadnezzar, Belshazzar, Darius, and Cyrus, rising to prominence in both the Babylonian and Persian empires. When he continued to pray to God, despite it being outlawed, he was thrown in with lions. Even facing the lions' den, he displayed unwavering faith by continuing to pray openly despite the royal decree against it.

Daniel received profound visions about future kingdoms and the Messiah, and his prophecies were extremely detailed. His life spanned the entire 70-year Babylonian captivity, and he lived to witness the first Jewish exiles return to Jerusalem following Cyrus's decree that exiled Jews may return to Jerusalem and rebuild the Temple.

Daniel's record reveals no major personal sin, though he carried the burden of his nation's exile. He confessed the collective sins of his people while maintaining personal integrity. His story highlights the challenges of living faithfully in a culture opposed to God's ways.

God blessed Daniel with wisdom, protection, and unusual longevity in royal service. Daniel received remarkable apocalyptic visions revealing God's plan throughout human history. His prophecy of the "seventy weeks" provided a timeline pointing toward Christ's arrival. Through consistent prayer and unwavering devotion, Daniel modeled how believers can engage with secular society while maintaining deep spiritual roots and staying faithful to God.

Daniel 6:10-11 (ESV)
'When Daniel knew that the document had been signed, he went to his house where he had windows in his upper chamber open toward Jerusalem. He got down on his knees three times a day and prayed and gave thanks before his God, as he had done previously. Then these men came by agreement and found Daniel making petition and plea before his God.'

Daniel 6:22 (ESV)
'My God sent his angel and shut the lions' mouths, and they have not harmed me, because I was found blameless before him; and also before you, O king, I have done no harm.'

DANIEL'S HISTORY IS RECORDED IN THE BOOK OF DANIEL.

Esther

Esther's Persian name means "star." Her Jewish name was Hadassah, meaning "myrtle" or "myrtle tree."

Esther was a Jewish orphan raised by her cousin Mordecai in Persia during exile. After King Xerxes removed Queen Vashti for defying his command, a kingdom-wide search began for a new queen. Esther was taken to the royal palace and eventually chosen as queen, though she kept her Jewish heritage secret at Mordecai's direction.

Haman, the king's highest official, harbored a deep hatred for Mordecai and devised a plot to destroy all Jews throughout the empire. When Mordecai learned of this scheme, he urged Esther to approach the king and plead for her people, reminding her that perhaps she had come to the throne for this very purpose.

Knowing that approaching the king uninvited could mean death, Esther asked the Jews to fast for three days while she did the same. Then, risking her life, she entered the king's presence. When he extended his golden scepter, granting her audience, she cleverly invited both the king and Haman to two special banquets.

At the second feast, Esther revealed her Jewish identity and exposed Haman's deadly plot. The king ordered Haman's execution and issued a new decree allowing the Jews to defend themselves, resulting in their survival and triumph.

Esther initially hid her Jewish identity and hesitated to risk her royal position to save her people. When first asked to intervene on behalf of her people, she showed reluctance to approach the king without invitation, requiring Mordecai's firm reminder about her unique responsibility. Her participation in Persian harem practices and palace protocols meant engaging in customs contradicting Jewish law. Her position as wife to a pagan king placed her in circumstances that tested her faith and cultural identity.

Esther 4:11 (ESV)
'All the king's servants and the people of the king's provinces know that if any man or woman goes to the king inside the inner court without being called, there is but one law—to be put to death, except the one to whom the king holds out the golden scepter so that he may live. But as for me, I have not been called to come in to the king these thirty days.'

Esther courageously risked her life for her people, recognizing that her royal position served a divine purpose. Her wisdom in approaching the king and confronting Haman's plot showed remarkable insight and self-discipline. Through her brave actions, God preserved the Jewish people from destruction, ensuring the continuation of the covenant line from which the Messiah would come. The feast of Purim, which Esther established with Mordecai, still celebrates God's deliverance thousands of years later, making her story one of the most enduring among Biblical women.

Esther 4:16 (ESV)
'Go, gather all the Jews to be found in Susa, and hold a fast on my behalf, and do not eat or drink for three days, night or day. I and my young women will also fast as you do. Then I will go to the king, though it is against the law, and if I perish, I perish.'

ESTHER'S HISTORY IS RECORDED IN THE BOOK OF ESTHER.

Anna
The Prophetess

Anna means "grace" or "favor."

Anna was an elderly prophetess who encountered the infant Jesus when Mary and Joseph brought him to the temple for consecration. She was the daughter of Phanuel from the tribe of Asher and had been widowed after only seven years of marriage. Following her husband's death, Anna dedicated herself entirely to temple service, where she remained for approximately 84 years. She spent her days worshiping through fasting and prayer, rarely leaving the temple complex.

When the infant Jesus was presented at the temple, Anna approached immediately after Simeon blessed the child. Recognizing the significance of this moment, she thanked God and spoke about Jesus to all, looking forward to Jerusalem's redemption. Her prophetic insight allowed her to identify Jesus as the long-awaited Messiah despite his humble appearance.

The Bible does not explicitly mention any moral failures or inequities committed by Anna. However, as a widow in ancient society, she likely faced social marginalization and economic hardship. The text suggests she lived during the oppressive rule of Herod and the Roman occupation, a time when many faithful Israelites struggled with doubt about God's promises, given their ongoing oppression. Though devoted to her service, Anna may have experienced periods of loneliness and doubt during her decades of temple service, waiting for the promised consolation of Israel by the Messiah.

Luke 2:37 (ESV)
'and then as a widow until she was eighty-four. She did not depart from the temple, worshiping with fasting and prayer night and day.'

After decades of faithful service and patient waiting, God granted Anna the profound blessing of witnessing the arrival of the Messiah before her death. This divine encounter represented the culmination of her life's devotion and validated her years of prayer and fasting. Despite her advanced age and the minimal status afforded to elderly widows in her society, God honored Anna by allowing her to be present at this pivotal moment in salvation history. Her faithfulness earned her the distinction of being one of the first evangelists, as she proclaimed the good news about Jesus to others awaiting redemption.

Luke 2:38 (ESV)
'And coming up at that very hour she began to give thanks to God and to speak of him to all who were waiting for the redemption of Jerusalem.'

ANNA'S ACCOUNT IS RECORDED IN LUKE 2:36-38.

Elisabeth

Elisabeth, or Elizabeth, means "God is my oath" or "my God is abundance."

Elisabeth was a descendant of Aaron, and the wife of Zechariah, a priest. Both were righteous people who faithfully followed God's commands. Despite their devotion, they remained childless into their old age.

While Zechariah served in the temple, the angel Gabriel appeared to him with news that Elisabeth would bear a son named John, who would prepare the way for the Messiah. When Zechariah doubted Gabriel's message, he was mute until the child was born. Elisabeth conceived as promised and recognized this as God's favor in removing her barrenness.

When her pregnant relative Mary visited, the baby in Elisabeth's womb leaped for joy. Filled with the Holy Spirit, Elisabeth became the first to acknowledge Jesus as Lord.

As John the Baptist's mother, Elisabeth's steadfast faith through years of waiting for a child, her quick recognition of God's work in her and Mary's life, and her obedience to divine instruction revealed spiritual maturity that influenced her son's powerful prophetic ministry.

Elisabeth followed all the Lord's commandments and statutes, and Scripture describes her as righteous and blameless before God. Unlike many Biblical figures, no specific sin is attributed to her. Yet, as a descendant of Adam, she inherited the sinful nature common to humanity, requiring God's grace. Her years without children, though not a sin, carried a heavy social stigma and personal burden that tested her faith deeply.

Luke 1:6-7 (ESV)
'And they were both righteous before God, walking blamelessly in all the commandments and statutes of the Lord. But they had no child, because Elizabeth was barren, and both were advanced in years.'

After years of childlessness, Elisabeth conceived in her old age through God's direct intervention. Her son, John, became one of history's greatest prophets, fulfilling Malachi's prophecy about the messenger who would prepare the way for the Messiah. When a pregnant Mary visited her, the Holy Spirit filled Elisabeth, making her the first person to recognize Jesus as Lord while He was still in Mary's womb. Her faithful waiting was rewarded not just with a son, but with a central role in God's plan of salvation.

Luke 1:41-43 (ESV)
'And when Elizabeth heard the greeting of Mary, the baby leaped in her womb. And Elizabeth was filled with the Holy Spirit, and she exclaimed with a loud cry, "Blessed are you among women, and blessed is the fruit of your womb! And why is this granted to me that the mother of my Lord should come to me?"'

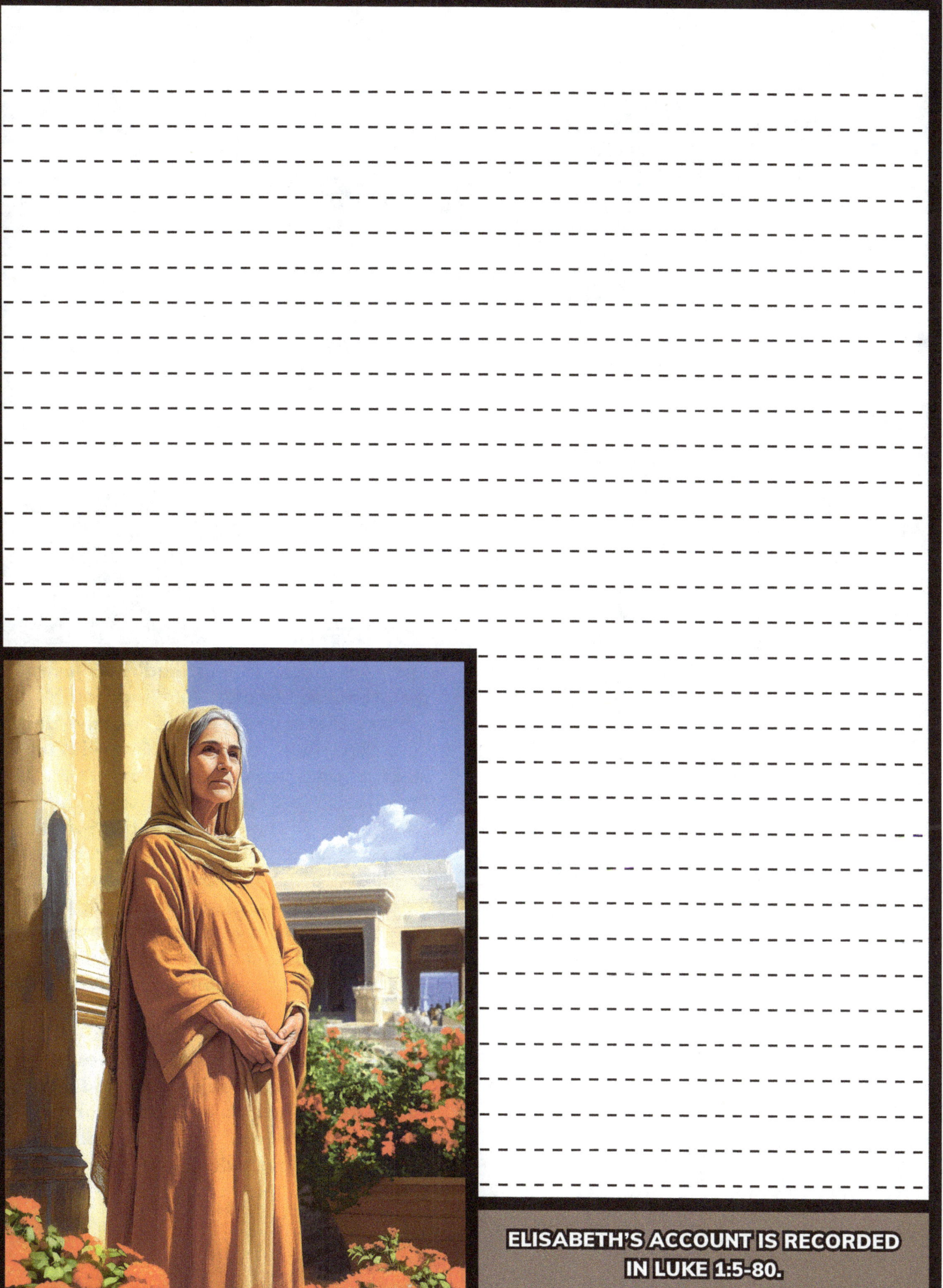

ELISABETH'S ACCOUNT IS RECORDED IN LUKE 1:5-80.

Mary
The Mother of Jesus

Mary is derived from the Hebrew name Miriam, meaning "bitter" or "rebellious."

Mary was a young Jewish woman from Nazareth, a small town in Galilee, engaged to a carpenter named Joseph. Her life changed when the angel Gabriel told her she had found favor with God and would bear a son through the Holy Spirit. This son, Jesus, would be the Son of the Most High and reign over Jacob's house forever. Despite the risks of an unexplained pregnancy, Mary accepted God's plan with humble faith.

While traveling to Bethlehem for a census, she gave birth to Jesus in a stable. Soon after, they fled to Egypt to escape King Herod's plot to kill the child, later returning to Nazareth, where they raised their family.

Mary appears at key moments in Jesus' ministry, including the wedding at Cana, where He performed His first miracle. Most importantly, she stood at the foot of the cross during His crucifixion, where Jesus entrusted her care to the apostle John. After Jesus ascended to heaven, she joined the disciples in the upper room, waiting for the Holy Spirit at Pentecost.

Scripture doesn't record major moral failures in Mary's life. However, like all humans except Jesus, she was born with a sinful nature and needed salvation. She felt worried and anxious when she and Joseph searched frantically for young Jesus in Jerusalem. On one occasion, she joined Jesus's brothers in trying to remove Him from a crowd when they thought He was "out of his mind," showing her limited grasp of His divine mission. These moments reveal her human struggle to trust God amid uncertainty.

Luke 2:48-50 (ESV)
'And when his parents saw him, they were astonished. And his mother said to him, "Son, why have you treated us so? Behold, your father and I have been searching for you in great distress." And he said to them, "Why were you looking for me? Did you not know that I must be in my Father's house?" And they did not understand the saying that he spoke to them.'

Mary was chosen to bear and raise Jesus, the promised Messiah, fulfilling Isaiah's prophecy that a virgin would conceive and bear a son called Immanuel, "God with us." She accepted this calling with trust and obedience to God's plan. Though she endured the pain of watching her Son die on the cross, her faith remained strong. As the mother of Jesus, Mary holds a special place in the story of salvation. Her life shows how faith grows through trusting God's Word, and as she foretold, all generations now call her blessed.

Luke 1:46-48 (ESV)
'And Mary said, "My soul magnifies the Lord, and my spirit rejoices in God my Savior, for he has looked on the humble estate of his servant. For behold, from now on all generations will call me blessed;"'

MARY'S ACCOUNT IS RECORDED IN MATTHEW 1 AND 2, MATTHEW 12:46-50, LUKE 1 AND 2, LUKE 8:19-21, JOHN 2:1-12, AND JOHN 19:25-27.

John the Baptist

John means "God is gracious."

John was born miraculously after the angel Gabriel appeared to his father Zacharias while he served as a priest in the temple, prophesying John's birth. His parents were elderly, and his mother, Elisabeth, was barren. John was filled with the Holy Spirit before birth, leaping in his mother's womb when Mary, pregnant with Jesus, visited.

John lived in the wilderness, wearing camel hair clothing and eating locusts and wild honey. His powerful preaching of repentance drew large crowds to the Jordan River, where he baptized many, including Jesus. He boldly proclaimed Jesus as "the Lamb of God who takes away the sin of the world."

Fearless in speaking the truth, John confronted King Herod Antipas for marrying his brother's wife, which led to his imprisonment and execution. Jesus declared that among those born of women, none was greater than John. His ministry bridged the Old and New Testament eras, fulfilling Malachi's prophecy of the messenger who would prepare the way for the Messiah.

Scripture doesn't record personal sin in John's life. While faithful to his calling, John experienced doubt during his imprisonment, sending disciples to ask Jesus if He was indeed the Messiah. His wilderness lifestyle and direct confrontation with Herod created social isolation and conflict. John struggled to grasp Jesus' ministry approach fully, expecting immediate judgment on the unrighteous rather than the patient grace Jesus often showed.

Luke 7:28 (ESV)
'I tell you, among those born of women none is greater than John. Yet the one who is least in the kingdom of God is greater than he.'

John was honored to announce Christ's arrival. He fulfilled Malachi's prophecy as the messenger preparing the way, connecting the Old and New Covenants. His ministry sparked widespread spiritual awakening through his call to repentance, preparing hearts for Jesus' message. Jesus called him more than a prophet and the greatest born among women. John received the unique privilege of baptizing the Messiah and witnessing the Trinity revealed in that moment.

Matthew 3:11 (ESV)
'I baptize you with water for repentance, but he who is coming after me is mightier than I, whose sandals I am not worthy to carry. He will baptize you with the Holy Spirit and fire.'

JOHN'S ACCOUNT IS RECORDED IN MATTHEW 3, 11 AND 14, MARK 1 AND 6, LUKE 1, 3 AND 7, AND JOHN 1 AND 3.

Martha

Martha means "lady" or "mistress."

Martha appears in Scripture as the sister of Mary and Lazarus. She is mentioned in three key Gospel passages. First, Jesus visited their home, where Martha busied herself with dinner preparations. While Mary listened to Jesus teach, Martha complained about her sister not helping. Jesus gently corrected her, saying Mary had chosen the better option.

The second account occured when Lazarus fell ill and died. Martha and Mary sent word to Jesus, but he arrived four days after Lazarus died. Martha met Jesus on the road while Mary stayed home, and her words to Jesus revealed both her raw grief and steadfast faith.

The final mention came shortly before Jesus' crucifixion. True to her nature, Martha served the dinner where Mary anointed Jesus with expensive perfume.

These glimpses of Martha's life show a woman of devotion, practicality, and deep faith. While often compared with her contemplative sister, Martha's forthright profession of faith and commitment to service highlight two vital aspects of following Jesus.

Martha became distracted by many tasks, missing precious moments with Jesus. Her worry over hospitality revealed her misplaced priorities. When she complained about her sister, Mary, not helping, she tried to control her sister and Jesus, showing a tendency to manage others rather than focus on what truly mattered. Her first words to Jesus after Lazarus died, "Lord, if you had been here, my brother would not have died," expressed faith but also contained a subtle criticism about his delayed arrival.

Luke 10:40-41 (ESV)
'But Martha was distracted with much serving. And she went up to him and said, "Lord, do you not care that my sister has left me to serve alone? Tell her then to help me." But the Lord answered her, "Martha, Martha, you are anxious and troubled about many things," '

Martha grew spiritually through her relationship with Jesus. When facing her brother's death, she made one of Scripture's most powerful faith statements: "Yes, Lord, I believe that you are the Christ, the Son of God, who is coming into the world." Jesus honored Martha by sharing with her one of his most important "I am" revelations: "I am the resurrection and the life." Martha witnessed her brother Lazarus return to life, experiencing firsthand Jesus' power over death. Her practical service became a genuine expression of love and discipleship.

John 11:27 (ESV)
'She said to him, "Yes, Lord; I believe that you are the Christ, the Son of God, who is coming into the world." '

MARTHA'S ACCOUNT IS RECORDED IN LUKE 10:38-42, AND JOHN 11 AND 12.

Mary Magdalene

Mary is derived from the Hebrew name, Miriam, meaning "bitter" or "rebellious." Mary's epithet, Magdalene, indicates her origin from the town of Magdala.

Mary Magdalene first appears in Scripture when Jesus freed her by casting out seven demons. Grateful for her healing, she became a devoted follower, supporting His ministry with her resources.

Throughout Jesus' ministry, Mary demonstrated unwavering loyalty. She stood at the cross during the crucifixion when many disciples had fled in fear. After Jesus' death, she carefully noted where His body was laid and returned after the Sabbath to anoint Him with spices, despite the danger of being associated with someone executed as a criminal.

Mary's defining moment came on resurrection morning. Finding the tomb empty at dawn, she ran to tell Peter and John. After they investigated and left, Mary remained, weeping outside the tomb. Jesus appeared to her first, and she recognized Him only when He spoke her name. He then entrusted her with telling the disciples about His resurrection, making her the first witness to this central truth of Christianity.

Before meeting Jesus, Mary Magdalene suffered under the oppression of seven demons, indicating severe spiritual bondage and profound personal suffering. The Bible does not detail her life during this possession, but such a condition would have brought social rejection and isolation. Her affliction likely caused behaviors beyond her control that violated social norms and God's design for her life. Like the other followers, when first encountering the risen Jesus, she failed to recognize Him, mistaking Him for the gardener in her grief and confusion.

Mark 16:9 (ESV)
'Now when he rose early on the first day of the week, he appeared first to Mary Magdalene, from whom he had cast out seven demons.'

Jesus completely freed Mary Magdalene from her demonic bondage, restoring her to wholeness. She was honored to be the first person to see the risen Christ and was commissioned as the first witness of the resurrection. In a society where women's testimonies carried little weight, Jesus deliberately chose Mary for this important role, forever linking her name with His resurrection. Her transformation reveals the life-changing power of an encounter with Christ.

John 20:16-18 (ESV)
'Jesus said to her, "Mary." She turned and said to him in Aramaic, "Rabboni!" (which means Teacher). Jesus said to her, "Do not cling to me, for I have not yet ascended to the Father; but go to my brothers and say to them, 'I am ascending to my Father and your Father, to my God and your God.'" Mary Magdalene went and announced to the disciples, "I have seen the Lord"—and that he had said these things to her.'

MARY IS MENTIONED IN MATTHEW 27:55-61, MATTHEW 28:1-10, MARK 15:40-47, MARK 16:1-11, LUKE 8:2, LUKE 24:1-11, JOHN 19:25, AND JOHN 20:1-18.

Peter

Peter originates from the Greek word Petros, meaning "rock." Jesus also called him Cephas, which means "rock" in Aramaic. His original name, Simon, means "God has heard."

Peter was a fisherman from Bethsaida who worked with his brother Andrew until Jesus called them to become "fishers of men." Jesus gave him the name Peter to signify his future role in the early church. As part of Jesus' inner circle with James and John, Peter witnessed pivotal moments like the Transfiguration of Jesus on the mountain.

Bold yet flawed, Peter made grand declarations of faith but also experienced dramatic failures. His leadership among the disciples was evident as he was the first to proclaim Jesus as "the Christ, the Son of the living God." Yet during Jesus' trial, fear overtook him, and he denied knowing Jesus three times. After the resurrection, Jesus restored Peter with a threefold command to "feed my sheep."

Following Pentecost, Peter led the early Jerusalem church with courage. He preached powerful sermons, performed miracles, and first brought the gospel to non-Jewish people. Roman tradition holds that Peter died in Rome during Emperor Nero's persecution, requesting to be crucified upside down because he felt unworthy to die as Jesus did.

Peter misunderstood Jesus' mission so profoundly that Jesus once rebuked him with, "Get behind me, Satan." When fear gripped him during Jesus' trial, Peter denied knowing his Lord three times, bringing him to bitter tears. His ethnic prejudice surfaced later, causing Paul to confront him publicly in Antioch. Peter's impulsive nature often led to hasty promises and actions, like cutting off a servant's ear in Gethsemane when soldiers came to arrest Jesus.

Luke 22:60-62 (ESV)
'But Peter said, "Man, I do not know what you are talking about." And immediately, while he was still speaking, the rooster crowed. And the Lord turned and looked at Peter. And Peter remembered the saying of the Lord, how he had said to him, "Before the rooster crows today, you will deny me three times." And he went out and wept bitterly.'

Jesus personally restored Peter after the resurrection, asking three times if Peter loved Him and commissioning him to care for His followers. At Pentecost, Peter preached boldly, and thousands believed, marking the church's birth. From fearful denier to fearless witness, Peter's transformation reveals how God's Spirit can overcome human weakness. The early church recognized him as a pillar of faith, and his two New Testament letters continue to guide and strengthen believers today.

John 21:17 (ESV)
'He said to him the third time, "Simon, son of John, do you love me?" Peter was grieved because he said to him the third time, "Do you love me?" and he said to him, "Lord, you know everything; you know that I love you." Jesus said to him, "Feed my sheep." '

PETER'S DENIAL OF JESUS IS DETAILED IN LUKE 22:54-62.

Matthew

Matthew means "gift of God" or "gift of Yahweh."
Levi means "joined" or "attached."

Matthew, also known as Levi, worked as a tax collector in Capernaum when Jesus called him. Tax collectors working for the Roman authorities were considered traitors by fellow Jews and excluded from religious life. His immediate response to Jesus' call showed a remarkable transformation, as he abandoned his profitable but despised profession to follow Christ.

He marked this life change by hosting a large feast at his home, inviting many tax collectors and social outcasts to meet Jesus. This gathering revealed both his joy in finding Christ and his eagerness to introduce others to Him. His occupation required literacy and accounting skills, abilities that later proved valuable when he authored the first Gospel.

Matthew's Gospel, crafted primarily for Jewish readers, repeatedly demonstrates how Jesus fulfilled Old Testament Messianic prophecies. He records many of Jesus' key teachings, including the complete Sermon on the Mount. Early church accounts tell us that Matthew preached in various regions, including Ethiopia, where some traditions suggest he died as a martyr.

Before following Jesus, Matthew worked in a profession marked by dishonesty and the exploitation of his own people. As a tax collector, he profited from an unjust system while serving Roman interests. His fellow Jews would have seen him as a traitor and social outcast. This reputation likely hindered his acceptance among the disciples and early Jewish believers.

Matthew 9:11 (ESV)
'And when the Pharisees saw this, they said to his disciples, "Why does your teacher eat with tax collectors and sinners?" '

Jesus invited Matthew to abandon his former life and become His follower. Matthew's swift response led to a complete transformation, bringing him into a life of purpose and truth. His Gospel uniquely highlights Jesus as the fulfillment of Old Testament prophecy, and his careful record of Jesus' teachings provides essential moral guidance for the church today. Matthew's journey from rejected tax collector to trusted apostle shows how Jesus redeems those whom society casts aside.

Matthew 9:9 (ESV)
'As Jesus passed on from there, he saw a man called Matthew sitting at the tax booth, and he said to him, "Follow me." And he rose and followed him.'

THE CALLING OF MATTHEW THE TAX COLLECTOR IS DETAILED IN MATTHEW 9.

Thomas

Both his Aramaic name, Thomas, and his Greek name, Didymus, means "twin."

Thomas was among the twelve apostles, though he's often remembered for doubting the resurrection. He first showed remarkable courage when he urged fellow disciples to follow Jesus to Bethany, willing to die with him if necessary.

Thomas was absent when Jesus appeared to the disciples after rising from the dead. He refused to believe that Jesus was alive unless he could touch Jesus's wounds, leading to a powerful encounter with Christ eight days later. His response, "My Lord and my God!" stands as one of the clearest declarations of Jesus' divinity in all the Gospels.

Early church tradition tells us that Thomas traveled east with the gospel message, reaching India, where he established several churches. It's believed he died as a martyr near Chennai (Madras), where his tomb became an important pilgrimage site. His journey shows how doubt can transform into deep faith through a personal encounter with Christ.

Thomas was absent when Jesus first appeared to the gathered disciples after the resurrection, and he refused to accept their testimony that Jesus was alive. His doubt led him to establish specific conditions for belief, effectively demanding God prove Himself on human terms.

John 20:24-25 (ESV)
'Now Thomas, one of the twelve, called the Twin, was not with them when Jesus came. So the other disciples told him, "We have seen the Lord." But he said to them, "Unless I see in his hands the mark of the nails, and place my finger into the mark of the nails, and place my hand into his side, I will never believe."'

Jesus met Thomas in his doubt without condemnation, inviting him to touch the wounds as he had requested. This divine patience transformed Thomas's skepticism into unshakable faith. His confession, "My Lord and my God," ranks among the strongest affirmations of Christ's deity in Scripture. Thomas later carried the gospel to India, showing how a former doubter became a bold messenger of truth.

John 20:27-28 (ESV)
'Then he said to Thomas, "Put your finger here, and see my hands; and put out your hand, and place it in my side. Do not disbelieve, but believe." Thomas answered him, "My Lord and my God!"'

THOMAS'S DOUBT IN JESUS' RESURRECTION IS DETAILED IN JOHN 20:24-29.

John

John means "God is gracious."

John, Zebedee's son and James's brother, was a fisherman when Jesus called him to be a disciple. He formed part of Jesus' innermost circle with Peter and James, witnessing pivotal moments like the Transfiguration and the raising of Jairus' daughter. In the Gospel bearing his name, John is described as "the disciple whom Jesus loved," revealing their special bond.

At the crucifixion, Jesus entrusted His mother, Mary, to John's care. After Jesus' resurrection, John became a pillar of the early Jerusalem church alongside Peter. Together, they healed the lame man at the temple gate and boldly proclaimed the gospel despite facing persecution. They later confirmed Samaritan believers had received the Holy Spirit.

John outlived all other apostles, enduring exile on the island of Patmos, where he received the visions recorded in Revelation. His writings, the Gospel of John, three letters, and Revelation, emphasize themes of love, light, and eternal life in Christ. Early church accounts place him in Ephesus during his final years, where he continued teaching about God's love until his death around AD 100.

John's record shows few personal failings. Early in his ministry, Jesus nicknamed him and his brother "Sons of Thunder," suggesting a fiery temperament. His occasional references to himself as "the disciple whom Jesus loved" might hint at a sense of special status. Yet, unlike many Biblical figures, John's story emphasizes faithful devotion rather than dramatic moral failures.

John enjoyed an exceptionally close relationship with Jesus, transforming him from an impulsive "Son of Thunder" into the "Apostle of Love." He confronted early church heresies threatening Christian teaching, particularly Gnosticism, denying Christ's humanity. Through his long life of faithful service, John provided the church with profound writings, culminating in Revelation's victorious vision of Christ's return and eternal kingdom.

John 21:20 (ESV)
'Peter turned and saw the disciple whom Jesus loved following them, the one who also had leaned back against him during the supper and had said, "Lord, who is it that is going to betray you?" '

John 1:14 (ESV)
'And the Word became flesh and dwelt among us, and we have seen his glory, glory as of the only Son from the Father, full of grace and truth.'

JOHN'S HISTORY IS RECORDED IN THE GOSPELS OF MATTHEW, MARK, LUKE, AND JOHN, AS WELL AS IN THE BOOKS OF ACTS AND REVELATION.

Stephen

Stephen means "crown" or "wreath."

Stephen was one of the seven men the early church chose to oversee the daily food distribution to widows. His selection required that he be "full of faith and of the Holy Spirit," and he was known for performing great signs and wonders among the people. His Greek name suggests he was a Hellenistic Jew, able to bridge the cultural gap between Hebrew and Greek-speaking believers.

When various Jewish groups strongly opposed his powerful preaching, Stephen faced false accusations. Before the Sanhedrin, he delivered a masterful defense, recounting Israel's history to show how they had repeatedly rejected God's messengers, culminating in their rejection of Jesus. His speech revealed his deep understanding of Scripture and its fulfillment in Christ.

As the first Christian martyr, Stephen's death profoundly impacted the early church. While being stoned, he saw Jesus standing at God's Right Hand and, like his Lord, prayed for his killers to be forgiven. His martyrdom sparked the first significant persecution of the church, scattering believers who spread the gospel beyond Jerusalem. Saul (later Paul) witnessed and approved of Stephen's execution, an event that likely influenced Paul's later conversion.

Stephen's bold confrontation of the religious authorities while facing false accusations intensified conflict with the Jewish leaders. Though blameless, his powerful speech challenged deep-seated traditions and triggered hostile reactions that brought severe persecution upon the vulnerable early church.

Acts 7:59 (ESV)
'And as they were stoning Stephen, he called out, "Lord Jesus, receive my spirit."'

Stephen became the first martyr for the Christian faith. His courage in the face of death honored God and inspired countless believers through the ages. Before dying, Stephen witnessed heaven open, with Jesus standing at God's Right Hand, a rare divine affirmation. His sacrifice catalyzed the spread of the gospel beyond Jerusalem, fulfilling Jesus's commission. Stephen's grace under persecution established a powerful model for Christian testimony amid suffering.

Acts 7:60 (ESV)
'And falling to his knees he cried out with a loud voice, "Lord, do not hold this sin against them." And when he had said this, he fell asleep.'

STEPHEN'S ACCOUNT IS RECORDED IN ACTS 6 AND 7.

Tabitha

Her Aramaic name, Tabitha, and her Greek name, Dorcas, means "gazelle."

Tabitha lived in Joppa, a coastal city near Jerusalem, where she served as a disciple in the early Christian community. She devoted herself to good works and helping the poor, earning recognition for her kindness.

She especially focused on making clothes for widows, who ranked among the most vulnerable people in ancient society. The community deeply valued her garment-making ministry, as became evident when she fell ill and died, causing widespread mourning among the believers in Joppa.

After her death, the community sent for Peter. Upon arrival, they showed him Tabitha's body and the clothes she had crafted. Peter asked everyone to leave the room, knelt and prayed, then said, "Tabitha, get up." She opened her eyes, saw Peter, and sat up. Her return to life led many people in Joppa to believe in the Lord, and she continued her compassionate service to others.

Scripture does not mention any personal flaws or moral failures in Tabitha's life. Her brief story highlights her faithful service rather than any shortcomings. Like all believers, she shared in the fallen human condition, but her narrative emphasizes her discipleship and good works instead. The only struggle recorded was her illness and death, which temporarily stopped her ministry to widows and the poor.

Acts 9:36 (ESV)
'Now there was in Joppa a disciple named Tabitha, which, translated, means Dorcas. She was full of good works and acts of charity.'

Tabitha received the extraordinary blessing of being raised from the dead through Peter's prayer, making her one of the few people in Scripture restored to life after death. Her resurrection became a powerful testimony that brought many in Joppa to faith in the Lord. Her designation as a disciple confirms her standing in the early church, showing how the community recognized women's vital contributions to ministry.

Acts 9:40-42 (ESV)
'But Peter put them all outside, and knelt down and prayed; and turning to the body he said, "Tabitha, arise." And she opened her eyes, and when she saw Peter she sat up. And he gave her his hand and raised her up. Then, calling the saints and widows, he presented her alive. And it became known throughout all Joppa, and many believed in the Lord.'

TABITHA'S ACCOUNT IS RECORDED IN ACTS 9:36-43.

His Latin name, Paulus, means "small" or "humble."
His Hebrew name, Saul, means "asked for" or "borrowed."

Paul, originally named Saul, was born in Tarsus to Jewish parents of the tribe of Benjamin. As a young man, he studied under the renowned rabbi Gamaliel in Jerusalem, becoming an expert in Jewish law and tradition. His passion for Judaism led him to persecute the early Christian church.

His life changed forever on the road to Damascus when the risen Christ appeared to him in a blinding light. After three years in Arabia, he began his work as the apostle to the Gentiles. He planted churches throughout Asia Minor and Greece through three missionary journeys, enduring persecution, imprisonment, and physical hardships.

Paul's letters shaped Christian theology and addressed real problems in early churches. His ministry blended deep thinking with heartfelt devotion to Christ, whom he valued above all his former accomplishments.

After years of service, he was arrested in Jerusalem and, after appealing to Caesar, was taken to Rome. According to tradition, he died as a martyr during Nero's persecution, likely by beheading as a Roman citizen.

Paul openly admitted his violent actions against believers before knowing Christ. His pre-conversion zeal for tradition had turned him into a persecutor who approved of Stephen's stoning. Paul wrote honestly about his ongoing battle with sin even after becoming a Christian, and he lived with a "thorn in the flesh" that remained despite his prayers for relief. He also experienced conflicts with other church leaders, including a notable disagreement with Barnabas about John Mark.

1 Timothy 1:15 (ESV)
'The saying is trustworthy and deserving of full acceptance, that Christ Jesus came into the world to save sinners, of whom I am the foremost.'

When Jesus met Paul on the Damascus road, he was transformed, becoming a powerful messenger of the gospel and builder of the church. His story proves that God can redeem anyone, regardless of their past. Paul wrote nearly one-third of the New Testament, giving the church its theological foundation. His travels established churches across the Mediterranean world, helping Christianity grow beyond its Jewish roots.

Acts 9:3-6 (ESV)
'Now as he went on his way, he approached Damascus, and suddenly a light from heaven shone around him. And falling to the ground, he heard a voice saying to him, "Saul, Saul, why are you persecuting me?" And he said, "Who are you, Lord?" And he said, "I am Jesus, whom you are persecuting. But rise and enter the city, and you will be told what you are to do."'

PAUL'S DRAMATIC CONVERSION ON THE ROAD TO DAMASCUS IS DETAILED IN ACTS 9. HIS HISTORY, FROM HIS CONVERSION TO HIS MISSIONARY JOURNEYS, ARE RECORDED IN ACTS 9 TO 28.

Lydia

Lydia was possibly named after her place of origin, Lydia, in Asia Minor.

Lydia was a merchant of purple fabric from Thyatira who lived in Philippi, a Roman colony in Macedonia. As a worshipper of God, she sought spiritual truth before encountering Christianity. She managed her own business and household, suggesting she held considerable status and independence in her community.

Paul and his companions met Lydia outside Philippi's city gates by the river, where women gathered for prayer on the Sabbath. As Paul shared the gospel, she listened intently, and God opened her heart to receive his message. She and her entire household were baptized that day.

Following her conversion, Lydia opened her home to Paul and his companions, providing them hospitality and a meeting place for the new believers in Philippi. Her home became the foundation for the Philippian church, which would later support Paul's ministry throughout his journeys.

Though Scripture mentions her briefly, Lydia's impact on early Christianity was profound as she helped establish one of Paul's most faithful and generous churches.

Scripture does not explicitly mention Lydia's personal flaws. As a successful businesswoman in Roman society, she likely faced tensions between commercial demands and her faith commitments. Though she worshipped God before meeting Paul, her spiritual journey remained incomplete until that pivotal encounter by the riverside. Her life hints at the universal human search for deeper meaning beyond material success. Despite her prosperity and social position, something was missing until "the Lord opened her heart" to receive Paul's message about Jesus Christ.

Acts 16:14 (ESV)
'One who heard us was a woman named Lydia, from the city of Thyatira, a seller of purple goods, who was a worshiper of God. The Lord opened her heart to pay attention to what was said by Paul.'

When the Lord opened Lydia's heart to Paul's teaching, her spiritual quest found fulfillment. As the first recorded European convert to Christianity, she played a crucial role in bringing the gospel to a new continent. Her immediate response was not just personal faith but generous action. By offering her home as both a shelter for missionaries and a gathering place for believers, Lydia demonstrated how God transforms individual lives to impact entire communities. Her resources became tools for kingdom work, showing that God often uses people's unique positions, skills, and possessions to advance His purposes in the world.

Acts 16:15 (ESV)
'And after she was baptized, and her household as well, she urged us, saying, "If you have judged me to be faithful to the Lord, come to my house and stay." And she prevailed upon us.'

LYDIA'S ACCOUNT IS RECORDED IN ACTS 16.